The
# EVERYTHING®
## College Survival Book
SECOND EDITION

Dear Reader:

When I began as a higher education administrator, the objective on my resume read: "To help undergraduate students get the most from their college experience and help first-year students adjust to college." My objective today is much the same. Working on this book gave me a chance to reach more students (as well as their families) and help them make the transition to college life.

The college years are probably the most anticipated, exciting, and rewarding of your young life. College is different from anything you have experienced thus far, and if you approach it carefully, you can get the most from these four fantastic years. Although each individual's experience is unique, there are themes common to all students. Whether you attend a research university or a liberal arts college, a school in a big city or one in the middle of cornfields, you'll benefit from the information presented in this book.

Take your time reading this book. Talk with friends and family about what you are reading and compare thoughts. Jot notes in the margins and bookmark the pages. Do whatever helps you prepare for this truly incredible experience: your college years.

*Michael S. Malone*

# The EVERYTHING® Series

## Editorial

| | |
|---|---|
| Publishing Director | Gary M. Krebs |
| Managing Editor | Kate McBride |
| Copy Chief | Laura M. Daly |
| Acquisitions Editor | Gina Chaimanis |
| Development Editor | Katie McDonough |
| Production Editors | Jamie Wielgus |
| | Bridget Brace |

## Production

| | |
|---|---|
| Production Director | Susan Beale |
| Production Manager | Michelle Roy Kelly |
| Series Designers | Daria Perreault |
| | Colleen Cunningham |
| | John Paulhus |
| Cover Design | Paul Beatrice |
| | Matt LeBlanc |
| Layout and Graphics | Colleen Cunningham |
| | Daria Perreault |
| | Monica Rhines |
| | Erin Ring |
| Series Cover Artist | Barry Littmann |

# THE
# EVERYTHING®
# COLLEGE SURVIVAL BOOK

**Second Edition**

From social life to study skills—
all you need to fit right in!

Michael S. Malone

Adams Media
Avon, Massachusetts

*This book is dedicated to my parents, Deborah and David Malone,*
*and to Greg Wells. Without their love, faith, and guidance,*
*I would not be in a position to write this book.*

An Everything® Series Book.
Everything® and everything.com® are registered trademarks of F+W Publications, Inc.

Published by Adams Media, an F+W Publications Company
57 Littlefield Street, Avon, MA 02322 U.S.A.
*www.adamsmedia.com*

ISBN: 1-59337-334-1
Printed in the United States of America.

J I H G F E D C B A

**Library of Congress Cataloging-in-Publication Data**
Malone, Michael S.
The everything college survival book / Michael S. Malone.-- 2nd ed.
p. cm.
(Everything series book)
Rev. ed. of: The everything college survival book / Jason Rich. 1997.
ISBN 1-59337-334-1
1. College student orientation--United States--Handbooks, manuals, etc.
I. Rich, Jason. Everything college survival book. II. Title. III. Series: Everything series.

LB2343.32.R53 2005
378.1'98--dc22

2004026913

This publication is designed to provide accurate and authoritative information with regard to the subject matter covered. It is sold with the understanding that the publisher is not engaged in rendering legal, accounting, or other professional advice. If legal advice or other expert assistance is required, the services of a competent professional person should be sought.
　　　　　　　—From a *Declaration of Principles* jointly adopted by a Committee of the American Bar Association and a Committee of Publishers and Associations

Many of the designations used by manufacturers and sellers to distinguish their products are claimed as trademarks. Where those designations appear in this book and Adams Media was aware of a trademark claim, the designations have been printed with initial capital letters.

*This book is available at quantity discounts for bulk purchases.*
*For information, please call 1-800-872-5627.*

# Contents

# Acknowledgments

Thanks first to Gina for gentle criticisms, generous compliments, and constant encouragement. Thanks also to Leslie for reading and rereading every word before it was finalized. Final thanks go to Linda, Mary, Rich, and Ruth for guidance in their areas of expertise.

# Top Ten Things to Do
# During Your First Year of College

1. **Find a favorite local restaurant:** Cafeteria food will get old before long, so find a place you and your friends can visit for an escape or a planned night out.

2. **Visit a new friend at his home:** Travel to see a different part of the country, meet a new college friend's family, and enjoy the break from classes.

3. **Bring a new friend home with you:** Show off your hometown, introduce your new friend to your family and high school buddies, and enjoy a favorite homecooked meal.

4. **Get to know the library:** Become acquainted with the campus library early in your college career and you'll see the benefits until the day you graduate.

5. **Send a thank you note home:** Write a heartfelt letter to your parents thanking them for all their love and support throughout your life. They'll treasure it for years to come.

6. **Visit your high school teachers:** Round up some friends, visit your old teachers and tell them about college. Thank them for helping you get there.

7. **Join a campus organization:** Get involved! Find an organization that interests you and attend meetings, plan events, and meet great new friends.

8. **Attend parties:** Gather a group of friends to dance, play games, or just hang out. Find your place in the social scene and balance out your study stress.

9. **Invite a professor to the cafeteria for lunch:** Your professor may be on campus for lunch anyway, so invite her to join you for a meal. Getting to know professors as more than just teachers is a great opportunity.

10. **Create (or revise) a resume:** Get assistance from your school's career office and prepare a resume that will impress future prospective employers. Starting early will get you on the path to a great job after graduation.

# Introduction

▶ After twelve years of formal education, the end is in sight. Yet in order to pursue your dreams and increase your earning potential you are about to head to college. Just an undergraduate degree means several more years of classes, papers, and tests. If you pursue a graduate degree, you could be in school for another six to ten years. And you are actually looking forward to this?

Of course you're looking forward to college! These will be the best years of your life so far. You will meet lifelong friends and perhaps your soul mate. You will try new things, learn valuable skills, and be challenged to figure out who you really are and what you stand for. You will fall in love with some of your classes (and perhaps classmates), deeply discuss serious issues with peers and professors, and enjoy many moments of quiet reflection.

You have achieved a lot and have done well to graduate from high school. You have learned what teachers want and how to succeed. However, college classes will move faster and your professors will be more demanding. You'll read thousand of pages and process dense information for class discussions and presentations. You'll also write hundreds of pages in essays, reports, and exams. To do so, you will spend many hours researching in the library, as well as many more hours studying in your room, in quiet places around campus, and even in the cafeteria.

As you are working harder and smarter than ever before, you will also be having more fun than ever before. There will be more concerts, parties, and cultural events than you have time to attend. You will have a full range of athletics to watch or participate in, nearby exercise facilities, and perhaps even natural resources such as hiking trails, beaches, or ski mountains to enjoy. You will meet and live with interesting people, some from places you have never visited, with very different backgrounds and expectations. By developing these new friendships, you'll learn more about yourself and what you want out of life.

By the time you finish college, you'll be prepared for a job in a field that may become a career. You'll also be prepared to change jobs if necessary, and you will still have college resources available to help you make that change. Your education in the classroom will be represented by your degree, but your education out of the classroom will shine on your resume and in job interviews. Leadership experiences, internships, and semesters spent abroad will all help shape your approach to life and your contribution to the adult world.

This book was written as a guide for you, as an incoming college freshman, and for your family. The topics covered in the following chapters will help you think about and prepare for the remarkable experience that is college. Each student's experience is different, but the themes students encounter are very similar, no matter what the size or location of the college. With a little thought and preparation, the transition from living at home and attending high school to living on your own and attending college can be a smooth one.

The experiences you have at college, in and out of the classroom, will not only help you personally and professionally upon graduation, but they will also help you determine your place in the world. The education and the great memories you leave with will be yours forever. Regardless of your background or future plans you are about to embark on a priceless journey. Good luck, and enjoy every minute!

## Chapter 1

# Financing Your Education

You have selected the schools you like most and have completed your applications. Though your acceptance letters and final decision may yet be months away, now is the time for you to figure out how you're going to pay for that college education. Few families have enough money to pay for a college education outright. You and your family will have to make some sacrifices, be a bit creative, and use a variety of methods to get the money needed to see you through several years of college.

## Financial Aid Offices and Forms

Your college's financial aid office will be one of the first to contact you after you are accepted to the school. Pay close attention to all communication from this office and be certain that you return all forms, filled out completely, by the deadlines indicated. No matter how thorough and vigilant you are, you'll surely have some questions about financial aid and the many forms you receive. Fortunately, you have a staff of experts at your disposal: your school's financial aid officers.

The financial aid officers at your school have an excellent understanding of student needs, federal regulations, and the paperwork necessary to receive financial aid. They have heard every question imaginable and understand that each student's situation may be unique. Financial aid officers also know of helpful resources available to students, including many outside of the college. Keep the financial aid office phone number posted on your refrigerator and try to speak to the same person each time you call. Your financial aid officer will usually remember your past conversations and can thus more accurately answer your new questions.

A common misconception is that you must be either very smart or very poor in order to receive financial aid. This is not even close to the truth. A variety of aid options exist for students of all levels of academic achievement and economic status. Search diligently and you will find something designed for someone in your situation.

Every student applying for financial aid must complete a Free Application for Federal Student Aid (FAFSA) form early in the calendar year. The FAFSA form standardizes much of the information colleges use to determine a student's expected family contribution and need. In addition, by late spring you must provide your school with a signed copy of your tax return, as well as your parents' tax returns. If your parents are separated or you have other special circumstances, get in touch with your financial aid officer to find out what forms are needed from each person.

Every aid application will require paperwork. Be certain that you keep copies of all the forms you fill out so that you can refer to them later. Keeping applications in separate envelopes or folders may help you find items quickly when you are on the phone asking questions or trying to figure out how much aid you have secured.

## *Searching for Grants and Scholarships*

Scholarships and grants are defined amounts of money that the college or another source gives to you for your educational expenses; these don't have to be repaid. Scholarships are the most sought-after type of aid for most college students. Scholarship eligibility is normally based on student characteristics, including one's academic merit, declared major, alumni relationship, and extracurricular involvement. Grants are different in that eligibility is based on the financial need of the student and family.

The federal government is probably the largest single source of financial aid for college students, typically focusing on need-based grants. But a surprising number of private organizations offer some sort of scholarship support as well. Take the time to search the Internet for possible financial aid opportunities. A quick search for "college scholarships" will turn up a wide variety of choices and possibly a lucrative award for which you are perfectly qualified. Also ask community agencies, such as churches and civic groups, if they have money available for students heading to college. Additionally, your family's employers may have grant programs for children or dependents of employees.

**ALERT!**

Several excellent scholarship databases are available for students, but you need to be cautious of any organizations that charge for their services. Some groups will try to sell you a list or have you complete an application so that you can be included in a database. Your search should not require either activity.

Local organizations are unlikely to give you large sums of money, but every little bit helps. For example, a few hundred dollars from a local civic group may fund your books for a semester. Find out about as many of these opportunities as possible and apply for any that you might be even remotely qualified for. Your goal is to gain as much grant and scholarship support as possible, even if it means getting a lot of small awards. You must notify your college financial aid office of any scholarships or grants that you obtain from outside sources. Be certain to ask your financial aid officer how outside scholarships and grants will affect your overall package.

Ask your financial aid officer what types of scholarships the school offers. Many alumni will endow a scholarship in memory of a loved one or favorite professor. You may find that there is a scholarship for students from your geographic region, planning to pursue your major, or any number of other special interests.

## *Maintaining Grants and Scholarships*

Getting grants and scholarships can be hard work, but don't take them for granted once you have received them. Some will be renewed automatically as long as you are continuously in school, but many will have to be applied for each year. In some cases, there may be strings attached to your scholarship or grant, such as maintaining a particular grade point average or continuing in a particular major or field of study.

There are a few basic questions you need to ask about each grant or scholarship you receive:

- Is the award renewable for each year that you are in college?
- What, specifically, do you have to do in order to maintain the award?
- Can the grant or scholarship be increased or decreased if your family's need changes?

Be cautious about one-time-only grants. Some colleges and organizations will offer students a scholarship or grant that is only good for the first year of college. If that award is not renewable, consider where you'll find that money for the rest of your time at college. You may find that the award is a bonus or that you can make up the difference with a small loan. But if the amount of the one-time grant is the last and irreplaceable piece of your financial aid package, you should talk to your financial aid officer about managing the costs of your second, third, and fourth years of school.

## *Leadership Development Awards*

Some financial aid awards are targeted to a specific area of study or development. A good example is scholarships that focus on leadership development. Local groups may have an interest in helping young people become leaders in the community. Organizations, such as a chamber of commerce, might have an award or know of local groups with that kind of money to give to deserving students. Some corporations enjoy the publicity that comes with helping to educate tomorrow's leaders, so be sure to avail yourself of any opportunities such companies may offer.

Don't be shy about your involvement and accomplishments when searching for financial aid. You are your own best promoter, and you need to talk about your qualifications confidently. Include positions you've held, groups of which you have been a member, and any community service you have done. Be confident in your approach and truthful about your qualifications.

Colleges often have scholarships designed to recruit or encourage student leaders. Eligibility will vary but often includes some demonstration of leadership in high school or your local community. However, colleges tend to think of leadership broadly, so don't rule yourself out if you were not the president of an organization or the captain of a team. Leadership is about making a difference, and that is exactly what the college wants you to do upon coming to campus. Some leadership awards will be based on your list of activities, some on an essay or application you complete, and some on interviews with college staff and students.

One of the best examples of leadership development aid is through the Reserve Officer Training Corps (ROTC) program. Students who choose to pursue this route for scholarship aid often find generous assistance for their education costs. However, if you receive money from an ROTC program, you'll be obligated to complete some sort of military service upon graduation. Most ROTC programs want to train the best leaders for today's military branches, and if they invest in helping you become a leader they will expect you to use that leadership to their benefit for a few years. The benefits of an ROTC program go beyond the scholarship money that is available. You can learn a number of new skills, meet some fascinating people, and develop a list of items for your resume that will be helpful when you begin a job search.

**ALERT!**

If you do receive an award from a company, community group, or other organization, it is appropriate to send each contributor a thank you note. Your note can be brief, but be certain that it is sincere. Let the groups know that you appreciate their support and that their gifts will be going to good use.

## Community Group Awards

Community groups know that educated individuals are the key to a healthy and prosperous community. These groups work to make communities stronger through service, sponsoring events, working with politicians, and sometimes giving college students educational grants. If a community organization contributes to your education, the members hope that you'll return to the community and be an engaged, positive contributor. Sometimes they recognize students who have been engaged in the community for several years, but just as often, community groups will recognize a student's potential to make a difference.

You must reach out to these groups and find out what scholarship or grant money they have available. When you call or visit organizations, be sure to ask if they have scholarship money that you can apply for or if they are aware of other groups in the community with such funds. When you find a group that supports college students, be prepared to submit an application including an essay detailing why you deserve the particular organization's support. You may also have to complete an interview with one or two staff members.

Churches and other worship centers frequently give financial support to members of their community. While the amount may be small, there are often perks associated with this kind of support. If everyone in the congregation knows that you are off at college, you may get the occasional care package from them, and when you come home for a visit many people will want to speak with you. It might also comfort you to know that a congregation is praying for your safety and success.

Remember that you are not alone in your search for financial aid. Ask your parents to inquire with their bosses and colleagues about opportunities that are available. Your high school guidance counselor, coaches, and teachers may also have some good leads. If you worked during high school, ask your boss for help—particularly if you worked for a national chain store.

## Work-Study Aid

Work-study aid is money from federal, state, and/or college sources that is available to you if you work on campus. These jobs can pose a great opportunity to work right on campus, learn more about a particular department that interests you, and form relationships with professors and other administrators, while earning money to fund your education. However, if you don't work the required hours, you could lose the opportunity and would then be forced to make up the money someplace else.

Your campus probably has a work-study office, often located in the financial aid office or career center. Contact this office to find out how to secure a job on campus. Be sure to ask if your campus guarantees jobs for students with a work-study award. Students with special skills, such as lifeguard certification, may be able to secure a desired job quickly. Other students will have to work hard to find lucrative positions on campus; the sooner you get started the better chance you have of finding a position. Don't rule out working for the college food service or maintenance programs. It may be hard work, but you'll meet some great people, students as well as staff, and have a lot of fun at the same time. Working for these offices can also have some nice perks, such as free leftover food or knowing which are the best residence halls on campus.

## *Loans*

Educational loans are a component of almost every financial aid package. They represent borrowed money that you or your parents must repay, usually with interest. The Federal Stafford Loan and Federal Perkins Loan are common low-interest loans available to students who have demonstrated financial need. Before your loan funds can be credited to your account, you must complete an entrance interview to learn about your rights and responsibilities. Your school may offer a group interview, you may be able to do this one-on-one with a financial aid counselor, or it may be possible to do this online.

An unsubsidized loan is a service as well as a product. It is in your family's best interest to shop around for the best loan for your situation. Your financial aid officer can give you good advice about what to look for in a loan, such as competitive interest rates and other terms.

Subsidized loans are based on a student's calculated need. If there is a difference between the cost of your education and your scholarships, work-study award, and your expected family contribution, then you will qualify for a subsidized loan. The government will pay the interest on the subsidized loans while you are in college or during grace periods. If the financial aid package your school offers you meets your demonstrated need, you will not qualify for subsidized loans.

Unsubsidized loans are need-blind, meaning that they are available to students regardless of individual or family need in relation to the cost of the college. However, the interest is not deferred—it accrues while you are in school, and any unpaid interest rolls over and is added to your loan principle. Because of this, unsubsidized loans tend to be more expensive than need-based loans and should probably be used as sparingly as possible.

Many loans are directed toward the student, but parents are often able to take on loans to help cover the difference between the cost of the education and the total financial aid offered. Parents may be able to borrow through a home equity loan or through the Federal PLUS program. PLUS loans have a variable interest rate and repayment of these loans must begin soon after the full loan amount is sent to the college. Families that take out loans to pay for a college education should check with a financial advisor or tax preparer to see if they qualify for a student loan interest deduction.

Students and families considering loans need to be careful about the balance between long-term debt and meeting education costs. Before you talk to a financial aid officer or other financial advisor, put together a list of questions about the loans you are considering. In addition to questions specific to your situation, be sure to ask:

- What are the terms of the loan?
- Is the loan subsidized or unsubsidized?
- How much will you owe by the time you graduate?
- What kind of monthly payments can be expected?
- What is the interest rate for the loan? Is it fixed or variable?
- Does the loan involve an up-front insurance payment or other additional fees?
- What is the maximum amount available from each lender?
- Are there any deferment or cancellation provisions associated with the loan?

It's very important for you to understand your complete financial aid package and how loans fit into the big picture. You want your loan debt to be manageable, so take advantage of every other opportunity, such as work-study or other employment, before relying on loans. When you do take on loans, do not borrow any more than you actually need.

**What if your first choice doesn't offer you enough aid to attend the college?**

Contact your financial aid officer and ask if there is an appeal process. Some schools will consider offers you've received from other colleges or recent changes in your family's specific circumstances. Be warned that state and community colleges typically have little flexibility in their offers.

## Cost Versus Value

Students head to college to further their education and to have an opportunity for a better life. The cost of an education is significant, but the value of a college degree is proven to be even more significant. When you are considering colleges, look at more than just the price tag for your education. The prestige of an institution, for example, or the acclaim of a particular department there, are intangible aspects that can affect the perceived worth of your degree. Remember, also, that the value of an education goes well beyond your experiences in the classroom.

As you compare your final list of schools, look at each very carefully. Ignore the prices for a moment and look at other indicators of value. These include:

- Qualifications and involvement of the faculty
- Class sizes and student to faculty ratio
- Specialized areas of study
- Opportunities to study beyond the campus
- Opportunities to use the latest technology
- Experimental education, such as study abroad opportunities
- Social life on and around campus
- Continuing services for alumni
- Placement of alumni in leading graduate programs
- Demonstrated success of alumni in the workplace

You may find that the college you deem most valuable is more expensive than you hoped, even if the school offers a generous financial aid package. In this case, you and your family must then weigh the immediate cost of loans against the total value of the education at that particular college. Looking only at cost will short-change your opportunity for an exceptional education and college experience. Likewise, judging less expensive schools to be providers of less valuable educations is unwise. Many community and state colleges provide educations competitive with the offerings of Ivy League schools for half the price. Do some research, talk to the experts, and make the decision that fits your needs and aspirations.

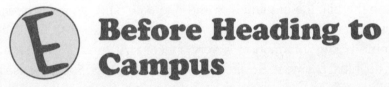

## Chapter 2

# Before Heading to Campus

O nce you have committed to a particular college, you'll be contacted by
various college offices on a regular basis.
You'll be congratulated, surveyed, and provided with key information to help you
make a successful transition to college life.
You may feel like the college is still courting
you, and in a way, it is. They want to prevent you from getting cold feet. However,
much of the information is important and
will help you get off to a good start at your
new school.

## Bills and Financial Materials

Few things are less exciting than a bill, and few things are more important. Keep all financial papers you receive from your college in one place so that you can keep track of and review them as necessary. As each bill arrives you need to read it carefully. Make sure you understand which office is sending the bill, the amount due and due date, and the consequences for late or missed payments.

Some billing information is very specific. At most colleges you must make an initial payment to hold your space in the class. You may also have to provide a deposit in order to guarantee housing. Additionally, you'll receive notices about optional health insurance and renter's or property insurance. In some cases, you'll be given the opportunity to opt out of some services and their related charges. It's important to note deadlines and penalty fees assigned to each bill. If you miss a particular payment, will you be charged interest on the amount due or assigned a fixed penalty amount?

**ALERT!**

Look carefully at each bill you receive and make sure that you are only paying legitimate bills. Your college will probably only send you a single bill for all official expenses, such as tuition, room, and board. Private companies may send you bills for services or products that you do not need or want. Read everything carefully.

Some of the bills you receive will be presented without particular explanation. However, each bill will include a phone number to call if you have questions. Don't hesitate to call this number to get an explanation of the bill, how it fits into the big picture of the cost of college, and what payment options you have. This is your first time through the process, so you may have questions. The person answering the phone has probably heard every imaginable question, so don't be shy or worry that your question is stupid. Anything that helps you understand this process is worthwhile.

In addition to keeping track of the materials you receive, you need to keep a record of payments you send out. If there is any question about when or whether you made a payment, you should be able to immediately tell someone what you paid, when, and other details of the transaction. While keeping track of this information may seem tedious, it will make your life much easier if difficulties arise. It will also help you get in the habit of managing your budget, which will be discussed further in Chapter 3.

## *Insurance and Health Information*

One of the earliest contacts you will receive will be from the college's health center. You will likely need to have a physical and provide proof that you have received various vaccinations. Look carefully at the due date for providing this information and make an appointment with your family physician accordingly. If you are unable to get to a doctor in time, call your college health center and see if they can provide the necessary services after your arrival to campus. Some items must be completed before you may begin classes or move into your residence hall, while others will be able to wait for a few weeks.

**FACT**

Meningitis is an inflammation and infection of the lining of the brain and spinal cord. Several states have passed laws requiring college students to provide proof of receiving or waiving a meningitis vaccination. Failure to do so may prevent you from registering for courses or moving into housing. Check with your campus health center to learn what is required of you regarding this vaccination.

You will also want to take this opportunity to let your school's heath center know about your special medical needs or conditions. If you have diabetes or asthma, for example, you need to let the professionals at the college know so they can further communicate how they can serve you. You also want to find out how to ensure that your personal physician can effectively communicate with the health center. You'll likely have to complete some additional forms to enable that communication. The important thing for you to learn is how the health center can help you meet your medical needs, either in their office or through community resources.

Most colleges have health care plans for students and will send information about those plans to you early in the summer. Read through the costs and benefits carefully, comparing the school's package to what you may be eligible for with your family's insurance. If you will use your family's coverage at school, check for eligible health care providers that are near your school. Your family's insurance may not cover you at college, in which case, some version of the school plan will be necessary. Many schools will automatically assign you their health insurance plan and require you to provide proof of alternate insurance if you want to opt out of their plan.

You also need to look into insuring your belongings. Colleges do not carry insurance that covers theft or damage to student property. Unless the school is negligent, which rarely happens, you'll be responsible for repair and replacement costs of damaged or stolen items. If your family's homeowner's insurance does not cover your belongings while you're at college, you should consider signing up for renter's insurance, either through a school-sponsored program or an insurance agency.

Petty theft occurs on most college campuses, and occasionally, a pipe leak, storm, or other problem will cause your belongings to be damaged. Record the serial numbers of all electronic equipment and make an estimate of the value of your books, clothing, and other belongings. When you speak with an insurance agent, talk about replacement cost for your belongings.

## Housing Decisions

Sometime between April and early June, you'll receive materials about housing on campus. Pay close attention to the forms you receive and dates by which you must return those forms to the school. In some cases, late return of the forms will mean that you are placed on a waiting list or are not eligible at all for campus housing.

One of the most important forms in this packet is the questionnaire that will be used to match you with a roommate. There are a few key pieces of advice you should heed when filling out these forms. First, fill out these forms by yourself. Parents often want to fill them out with you or even complete them on your behalf, but it is important that this information represents you and your preferences. Second, be completely honest. If you smoke, say so—even if your parents don't know it. If you truly like classical music, mention this, even if you've been made fun of for it in the past. Third, remember that the survey is a snapshot of you at this moment. By November you will have changed and may answer the survey differently. The same will be true for your roommate. You will each start on similar footing and will change over the course of the semester. Be prepared to manage these changes.

**ALERT!**

Every year students fill out housing surveys honestly and thoroughly and still find that their roommates don't become their best friends. This is normal. Surveys help your housing office match students with a few similar interests, but you will inevitably find more differences. Your goal is to learn how to live with this new person, even if you do not become best friends.

Some schools will give you the opportunity to request a particular roommate. However, almost every housing professional you can ask will advise against selecting a friend as a roommate. Living with a friend is much different than hanging out with him. College may seem like a large and unfriendly place—intimidating to someone new. But rather than live with your friend try to live near him. You will benefit more from having another room to visit and the two of you may make twice as many friends by living apart. You will also be free to be yourself, even if that means being different than you were in high school. Most importantly, you'll preserve a valued friendship.

If you are given the opportunity to request a particular residence hall, consider your choices carefully. One hall may appear to have better amenities but is actually located on the fringe of campus. Some buildings will have traditional rooms with shared bathrooms; others will be arranged in suites with bathrooms shared only by a handful of people. Most buildings will house men and women, sometimes on the same floor, while others will be for one gender only. Think about your daily life and your preferences when choosing a particular hall, and resolve to make the best of whichever hall you eventually choose.

Some colleges have begun offering new students the chance to live in learning communities. These groups are usually housed together on one floor of a residence hall or in a suite-style building. Most learning communities are organized around a particular class or special interest, such as leadership, multiculturalism, or service. Choosing a learning community often means agreeing to participate in extra work outside of class, including workshops, field trips, and discussion groups in your residence hall. However, early research shows that students who participate in learning communities are more likely to stay at their college and report higher levels of satisfaction than those who do not. Learning communities are not for everyone, but they are worth serious consideration.

## *Orientation Materials*

Your first major event as a college student will be orientation. The orientation office will begin sending you information about particular programs, dates, and costs sometime in the spring. Pay attention to the particular details and options involved with orientation. Is orientation held in the summer or just prior to the start of classes? Is there one orientation for everyone or specific sessions for specific individuals? When do you need to arrive and where will you be staying?

Some of your orientation sessions will seem dry, pointless, or just plain corny. Attend everything regardless of these perceptions. Students and professionals have put these sessions together for a good reason. At the very least you and your new friends will have something to laugh at and complain about together.

Most orientation programs try to accomplish three broad goals. First, the program tries to orient you to campus. You will need to know where to find your classes, where the library and computer labs are, where to find and how to use the fitness center, etc. Second, orientation will formally introduce you to expectations of college life. Academic expectations, conduct policies, and school traditions will be covered. Third, the orientation program will help you get to know your classmates and begin building friendships that may last the rest of your life.

The information you receive about orientation may include a common reading. Some schools require all new students to read a book or set of articles prior to arriving on campus. Often, the school will provide these materials for you; sometimes you will have to purchase them yourself. It's important for you to complete this reading. While it does represent homework over the summer, which was probably not on your list of things to do after high school graduation, it's your first academic assignment from the college. You and your peers at college will have this reading as a shared experience, and you will probably be asked to discuss the material or reflect on it in writing. You may also be asked to relate the common reading to something you are discussing in one of your classes. Take this assignment seriously and give yourself plenty of time to complete and understand the material.

**ALERT!**

Pay careful attention to directions provided in your orientation materials. When arriving on campus for move-in day, you may have to report to a particular area first. Also, since hundreds of other students will be moving in at the same time, your campus is likely to have particular directions for unloading your belongings and parking the family car.

You need to approach much of orientation seriously. If you learn things at this time, such as how to use the library effectively, you will not have to relearn them later. But also come to orientation prepared to have fun. Keep an open mind and be careful to not judge others quickly. Your classmates will be as nervous and excited as you are and in the rush to impress everyone it is easy to start forming cliques. It's also easy to make mistakes, so forgive yourself and others quickly if that happens. Get to know as many people as possible and be friendly to everyone.

Some colleges have a special or preorientation option for new students. These programs often involve outdoor experiences, such as hiking, bicycling, or taking advantage of natural resources close to campus. Other programs focus on community service projects. Often there is a small additional cost associated with these programs, and sometimes there are scholarships or fee waivers available for highly motivated but financially strapped students. Consider these special orientation programs carefully. In addition to the value of the specific program, you are able to move into your residence hall early and get to know a small group of people before the entire class arrives. For many students, this is an excellent transition to college. Participation in a preorientation program could be the first step to becoming president of an outdoors club or a member of a service fraternity.

## Who to Call with Questions

Colleges put a lot of effort into making their communications self-explanatory and complete. But they also know that this is your first time through the process and some things may not make sense to you initially. From time to time, you may have a question or particular circumstance not answered in the materials that you receive, or what you receive may only confuse you. The quickest and easiest way to get the information you need is to call someone at the college.

The first place to call is the office that sent you the information that created the question. If you have a question about your bill, call the number listed at the top or bottom of your bill. If you have a question about health insurance forms, call the health center. These offices probably hear your particular question regularly and can provide you with a quick answer.

If your question isn't obviously attached to a particular office, there are two places to call. The orientation office can usually field a wide variety of new student questions. If they're not able to answer your question, they can usually transfer you to the correct office. Not only are they expecting most phone calls to be questions from new students, they are cheerful and eager to be helpful. The other office you can call is the admissions office. Although you are no longer a prospective student, they still want to help you with your transition to college. They may be able to answer your particular question, but if not, they can quickly transfer your call to the office that can help.

When you were considering various colleges, a student may have called you offering to answer any questions you have. You may also remember your student tour guide from your campus visit. Look up these students in your college's online directory and contact them for answers to your questions. They will probably be flattered that you remembered them and happy to help you out.

## Friends and Family

The few months before college are a great time to start your own address book. As high school graduation comes and goes, you'll receive cards from friends and family. Set these aside and treat them as a starting point for your address book. These people are already involved in your life, are interested in hearing about how you are doing, and are likely to send you mail at college.

Once you know your college mailing address, send a brief note or postcard to everyone in your address book. Include your mailing address, college e-mail address, and residence hall phone number. Add a few lines about why you are excited about attending this particular college, and thank each person for their continued support in your life. This brief note from you may inspire letters and packages for your birthday, holidays, or for no particular reason. And receiving mail from family and friends can help make you feel even more comfortable in your new college life.

Once you get to college, take some time each week to send one or two people a brief note or card. Be certain to remember family and friends' birthdays, anniversaries, and other important dates. They will be glad to know that you have not forgotten about them even though you are becoming more independent. You might also ask these people for advice from time to time; it's a good idea to get tips from people you trust while you're getting settled. And hopefully, a quick note from you will inspire each of them to send you a letter in return.

A card or e-mail is a good way to stay in touch with most of the people listed in your address book, but don't forget about the phone. You should call your parents at least once a week to tell them how you are doing, find out how things are at home, and keep up on family news. It is also worth calling grandparents and good friends once in a while. Nothing can replace a one-on-one visit, but hearing a familiar voice can comfort you both.

**QUESTION?**

**What if I don't like the cafeteria food?**

Unfortunately, college cafeterias don't always have a wide selection and may not carry foods you're used to. To keep eating comfortably without breaking your budget, ask a parent or relative to send a favorite treat from home. Whether it's a batch of your mother's brownies or a fruit basket from your aunt, an extra treat from a loved one can help you make this transition.

*Chapter 3*

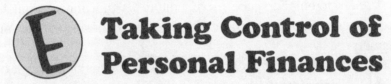

# Taking Control of Personal Finances

You've been told that being an independent adult comes with responsibility. One of the first big responsibilities you are about to assume is primary responsibility for your personal finances. You will have to make significant decisions that will affect your day-to-day life, as well as your future. When developing a budget, you will quickly learn what works for you and what does not.

## Cash, Credit, or Check

Although your basic needs are taken care of and you brought a lot of personal items from home, you'll eventually find yourself needing money for some extra purchases. You will buy essentials such as books, lab supplies, and pens. You'll also go out to eat, go see or rent movies, and go to concerts. The key to balancing these expenditures is knowing how much money you have at all times, sticking to a budget, and choosing the best method of payment.

Cash in small amounts is the most popular means of payment on and around a college campus. You don't want to carry around hundreds of dollars or leave that much money hidden in your residence hall room, but you want to be able to purchase a cup of coffee on the way to class or go off campus for lunch with classmates. The big advantage to cash is that it is accepted everywhere and doesn't cost you anything in terms of interest fees or finance charges.

**FACT**

Some colleges allow you to charge things internally, placing the charge directly on your bill. With this option you don't have to part with any of your pocket cash or add a charge to your credit card, but your parents will likely see the bill and wonder just what they are paying for. If you use this method at all, do so with caution.

Checks are a popular means for more expensive purchases. You will not have enough cash on hand to purchase all of your books for the semester, and your campus bookstore is likely willing to accept a personal check. Off-campus, you may have trouble using checks to pay for items, and if you write too many checks you may incur extra fees through your bank. But if you are going to write checks for purchases, be prepared to show a driver's license or other form of identification.

Many students use credit cards to purchase anything from books to items from the convenience store. Credit cards have the advantage of being accepted almost everywhere, including Internet shopping sites. Still, some stores and restaurants require a minimum purchase amount before you can charge items. Credit cards are more complicated than cash or checks and warrant some extended discussion.

## *Credit Cards: Pros and Cons*

When you get ready for college, the issue will not be so much how to get a credit card as *which* credit card to get. Advertisements will be stuffed in your bookstore bags, companies will send solicitations to your campus mailbox, and there will be fliers posted all over campus. There are good reasons to have a credit card, namely for emergencies, for travel, and to keep from carrying large amounts of cash. However, there are a number of pitfalls as well.

Some credit card companies will give you something free just for signing up for their card. You may receive a free item on the spot, they may mail you something once your application is approved, or they may "forgive" your membership fee. Be wary of such offers. If they are willing to give you something for free, what's in it for them? Read the fine print to be sure.

If your bankcard also works like a credit card, you may not need anything else. Such cards are accepted like any credit card, but the charge is deducted from your checking account. One advantage of this arrangement is that you are unlikely to incur finance charges. However, you are also not going to build a credit history. Using your bankcard as your primary charge option might be a good idea, but you should consider having a traditional credit card as well.

It's important to compare credit card offers carefully and read all of the fine print before making a decision. A 0 percent annual percentage rate (APR) looks great but may only last for a limited time. The lower your fixed APR, the better it is for your budget. In addition to APRs, you should look at annual fees. Many cards charge you for the privilege of using their services.

**ALERT!**

Most credit cards allow you to make charges or get cash advances, and the latter deserve particular caution. Cash advances are usually subject to a transaction fee and sometimes a higher interest rate. Also, your cash advance limit is often lower than your total credit limit. Use your credit card sparingly and for charges only, if possible.

Remember that charging something actually increases its cost if you don't pay your credit card bill immediately. Missing payments or carrying a large balance can also hurt your credit rating. A damaged rating takes time to repair, and when you graduate you may find that you need a good credit rating to get yourself established in the next phase of your life.

Plan on getting only one card, and find one with a low credit limit. You won't need more than a $1,000 limit even in emergencies, so anything more than that may do more harm than good. Also, try not to carry your card with you at all times. If you don't carry the card regularly, you will be less likely to make impulsive purchases. Finally, be careful about using your credit card for online purchases. While this is an easy way to shop, online security is always a concern.

## Finding a Local Bank

Many students and their families decide that the student should have an account with a bank in the town where the college is located. However, this may not be necessary. If you rarely use a bank at home, you may not use a bank often while at college either. Perhaps the college has a check cashing service or a safe to hold large sums of cash. You can certainly use those services and survive well at college, but check with your campus first to learn just what services they provide, as well as the limitations of those services.

One of the advantages of having a local bank is access to a full range of banking services and the ability to meet with bank staff when needed. It also gives each student that much more control of her financial health and can be an excellent educational tool. Since banks usually have ATMs near campus, students will have twenty-four-hour access to their money, which is especially important when your friends decide to take a late-night trip for food or to visit another college.

Your experience finding a bank will vary depending on whether you are in a big city or a small town. The larger the town, the more banks will be available. You may find that your home bank has a branch near your college through which you can access your existing account. You may also find that your college conducts business with a particular bank and has arrangements to help students bank there. Both cases can make your life a little easier.

Most college students don't actually go into a bank often during their college careers. You will be able to conduct most of your business online, through ATMs, and by mail. However, it's a good idea to have a branch near campus for those rare occasions when you need immediate assistance with a banking issue.

If you are going to start an account with a new bank, you need to understand the various account packages offered and how they fit with your banking needs. For example, you are unlikely to need unlimited checking if most of your spending will be with cash or credit. Here are a few questions to ask before opening an account:

- What is the interest rate for each account?
- Is there a charge for writing checks?
- Do you have to maintain a minimum balance on each account?
- What is the charge for bouncing a check?
- Can you link checking and savings accounts for overdraft protection?
- How often will you receive statements?
- Is there an extra charge for getting or using a bank (ATM) card?
- Can your ATM card be used like a credit card?
- Where are other branches of the bank?
- Where are the bank's ATMs located?

## *ATMs*

ATMs can be found almost everywhere these days. They offer convenient access to money in stores, malls, gas stations, airports, and just about any other place people are likely to spend money. Consequently, it is highly probable that you'll have ATMs on or very near your campus. You can use these machines, as well as online banking services, to conduct much of the business you have with your bank.

**FACT**

Many banks now offer online services for their customers. These services will allow you to check your balance, see a history of transactions, stop payment on checks, and even submit a loan application from the comfort of your own computer. In addition, since these services are available twenty-four hours a day, you can use them when it is convenient for you.

Use of ATMs comes with a few warnings. First, if your bank or network does not own the ATM you are using, there might be an extra charge for using that machine. Charges usually range from $0.50 to $2.00 per transaction. Keep in mind that frequent use of such ATMs will quickly deplete your bank account. Find an ATM that's in your network instead of regularly using machines that charge the extra fee. If you do use a machine that charges a transaction fee, be certain that you include that fee when you balance your checkbook.

A second caution for ATM use is security. While most ATMs are in well-lit areas and are monitored by videotape, you still need to exercise caution at these machines. Shield the keypad when you enter your PIN code so that nobody can look over your shoulder. Be aware of who is around you while you are at the ATM, and don't count your money out in the open, where others can see how much you have withdrawn.

## *Living on a Budget*

You don't have to be an economics major to understand that your spending cannot outpace your income. Now that you are in charge of providing everything beyond your basic necessities, you need to establish a budget and stick to it. Parents are a good resource when you begin thinking about budgeting. Not only are they already familiar with your finances, they have managed a larger and more complex budget for an extended time.

**QUESTION?**

**Are there any special discounts available to college students?**
Absolutely. Many stores, restaurants, movie theaters, and auto shops near your college will likely offer student discounts. You'll simply need to present your student ID when you make your purchase.

You probably don't need a detailed budget for college life. Instead think of general categories of spending and set an amount for each. After you have listed each category, total the amount you anticipate spending and compare that with your income and savings. If you're spending more than you're making, you need to find places where you can spend less. Some categories you should consider for your budget are:

- Travel to and from home
- Travel around town
- Car maintenance and gasoline
- Eating out and food deliveries
- Entertainment, such as movies and concerts
- Clothing purchases
- DVD/CD purchases
- Phone bills
- Holiday and birthday gifts
- Laundry
- Toiletries and medications

Once you get to college, keep track of where your money is going. For example, if you take money from an ATM record what you used it for. This will help you make adjustments to your budget when necessary. You should also build in some cushion for emergencies or spontaneous moments. Finally, be prepared to say "no" to some activities. You simply can't go out to eat every night, go to every concert, or do other things that drain your budget. Finding no-cost entertainment won't be hard once you decide not to spend more money.

# Big Purchases

You'll spend plenty of time and money on small purchases—things you need to carry out everyday life—so it is important that you give big purchases a lot of thought. If they are well planned, big purchases can be worth every cent. To buy wisely, you should do research and carefully weigh your "need" opposite your desire. Additionally, if you seriously consider all big purchases, you will most likely take better care of these investments in the long run.

## The Car Question

Cars are one of the most expensive items you can purchase before heading to campus. Not only do you have to consider the cost of the car, complete with license and registration, you need to consider insurance and maintenance costs. Few people are able to purchase a car outright, which means that you will likely have to get a loan and make monthly payments. These things will eat heavily into your budget.

On small college campuses, you can usually walk from residence halls to classes and to the cafeteria in a few minutes. On larger campuses, you will probably have access to buses or shuttles. During break periods, you can hitch a ride with a friend or use public transportation. One of your friends at college is likely to have a car and will take trips to local malls, movie theaters, and restaurants. In short, you probably won't need a car during your first year of college. Deciding against having a car will save you money and time you need for other things.

A good place to start researching big purchases is *Consumer Reports*. You can find copies at bookstores and libraries or find it on the Internet at ✐*www.consumerreports.org*. A nonprofit group whose mission is to test products, inform the public and protect consumers publishes *Consumer Reports*. It doesn't accept commercial sponsorship or endorsement, so findings are considered to be objective.

If you decide to purchase a car, research the models that you are considering. Pay special attention to safety records, maintenance records, and gas mileage estimates. Before making a final purchase talk to an insurance agent to get a rate estimate for the different cars you are considering. Decide which amenities, such as power windows or air-conditioning, you can do without in order to help keep the cost down. And, as with other big purchases, seek the advice of family and friends who have experience purchasing cars.

## Computers

In recent years, the computer has become a staple of college life. However, that doesn't mean you have to own a computer before getting to campus. Most campuses have multiple computer labs with extended hours, printers, and technical support staff on hand. Many colleges have a shared hard drive so that you can access your files from any computer on the campus network. It may be in your best interest to delay purchasing a computer until after you are on campus and know what your computing needs really are.

Once you decide to purchase a computer, you need to make a few choices. The first is to pick a computer platform, typically a Macintosh- or Windows-based computer. If your campus has not already told you what platforms it supports, you should call and ask. You also need to consider how you will be using the computer. Some academic majors rely more on one platform than the other.

The next choice you typically need to make is between a desktop and laptop computer. Laptops are highly portable and can go with you to class, the library, and your residence hall room. Many colleges are installing wireless networks that enhance your ability to use a laptop all over campus. However, the portability of laptops makes them an easy target for thieves. Laptops also tend to need upgrades more frequently than desktop computers.

Regardless of the type of computer you choose, you need to purchase a package that meets your computing needs. At a minimum you will need word processing, Internet and e-mail, and virus protection packages. For some classes you may need spreadsheet, publishing, or statistic-processing software. If you plan to play games on your computer you will want to pay attention to sound and graphics capabilities. Similarly, if you are going to play or record music or movies you will need the appropriate software for these activities.

**ALERT!**

Most colleges have requirements you must meet before you are permitted to plug your computer into the college network. These range from concerns about network security to virus prevention. Call ahead and make sure you know what will be expected in order to use the campus network.

Many stores sell basic computer systems and most offer some type of financing for your purchase. Some companies, such as Dell and Gateway, market their ability to customize a computer system to your particular needs. Your campus bookstore may also offer special deals or have a relationship with particular manufacturers. Explore all of these in order to get the maximum computer system for the minimum price.

## Choosing Electronics

Your residence hall room will be your home for a few months, and you are going to want every luxury you can squeeze into that small space. But you should keep in mind that the college environment is one of high wear and tear for items, so spending your life's savings on an entertainment system is probably not the best move.

Many students bring game systems to campus. These can provide great sport in residence hall rooms and lounges. Late nights and weekends are often filled with video game tournaments, and sports games are particularly popular in residence halls. So, if you already have a game system and you are willing to let a lot of people use it, you may consider bringing it to college. If you do not have a game system, however, don't go out and buy one just because you are going to college. Even if your roommate doesn't have one, someone else on your floor is bound to. In addition, every couple of years a new and better game system comes on the market. The game system you purchase now will be obsolete before you graduate from college.

Many residence hall rooms are not air-conditioned, but most campuses do not allow students to bring their own window air-conditioning units. If you require air-conditioning for health reasons, get in touch with your campus health services office as soon as possible. Otherwise, consider a window fan or an oscillating fan that you can move around the room.

Most students own a portable music device such as a CD player or iPod. These are useful in a variety of ways. You can easily take your music with you to the library, to work out, to your favorite study space on campus, and on trips to and from home. You can also use your headphones when you don't want to disturb your roommate or you want to block out some noisy neighbors. If you're going to purchase a portable music device consider cost, size, and compatibility with other electronics you own. The iPod, for example, stores a large amount of music and can work with most computers, in cars (with an adapter), or on its own. However, it's more expensive than a portable CD player or radio.

Finally, there is always the question of microwaves and refrigerators. These items have become standard components of the modern residence hall room. Most colleges have a rental plan for combination refrigerator/microwave units. The advantage of renting is that you don't have to haul the unit to and from college and if it breaks the college will replace it quickly at no cost to you. The disadvantage is that over three or four years, it's cheaper to purchase your own units.

Before you decide to purchase a refrigerator or microwave, read the material from your housing office. Some campuses prohibit cooking in dorm rooms, including microwaves and coffee makers. Most schools have a restriction on size and electricity usage for refrigerators as well.

## Cell Phones

It may seem to you that every college student has a cell phone. However, while cell phones are good to have in emergency situations, you do not necessarily *need* one. You will have phone service in your residence hall room and the option to have a long distance phone plan through the college, as well. Regardless of the service you select for your residence hall room, you'll be able to use it to receive calls and make calling card calls.

**ALERT!**

Cell phones come with some less obvious drawbacks. For example, if you walk across campus constantly talking on your cell phone, you miss the opportunity to interact with people around you. Also, if your cell phone rings during class, you will not impress your professor. Be aware of when and how you are using your cell phone.

If you currently have a cell phone and plan to keep it at college, check with your provider about the availability of service at your campus, changes to your plan that may be necessary, and the dealer location that is closest to campus. If you don't have a cell phone but decide that you need one, you need to do some research. Start by asking people at your campus what carrier most students use and if they are aware of problems with any of the major carriers. Then decide what you will need in a phone. If you just need to call family occasionally, you can get a basic phone and a cheap plan. If you need to use your phone as a personal organizer, e-mail station, camera, and as your primary phone, you will need to spend considerably more money. Most students will have needs that fall somewhere between these extremes.

Once you have an idea of what you're looking for, visit several cell phone dealers. Get written descriptions of the plans they offer and look at all the types of phones they have. Ask questions about rebates, areas of service, changing plans, and leaving that provider. You also want to ask about service. If your phone is damaged will a local dealer give you a new phone while yours is being repaired? How long do repairs take? How long does the battery last, and what does the phone manufacturer consider to be "normal use"?

Cell phones are evolving quickly and offer myriad extras. When a sales clerk starts telling you about all of the extra features of a particular phone or plan it is easy to get caught up in all the options. Try to keep in mind that those fun extras cost extra as well. Stick to a phone that provides you with the basic needs you identified before you began shopping.

# The Important Details

Though your new financial responsibility can be stressful, there are a number of things you can do to make this transition easier on yourself. The best way to maintain control over your financial matters is to record your purchases, stay familiar with your checking and savings accounts, and use your credit cards judiciously. If you always know how much you've spent and how much you have, scary surprises should not happen often. It is also important to do the essential (though often tedious) chores that will help you maintain your budget. Be sure to do things like balance your checkbook, and become as educated as possible about commonly gray areas, like credit reports.

## Balancing Your Checkbook

Balancing your checkbook may be one of the most unromantic chores you will ever undertake. It is also one of the easiest things you can do to keep your life in order and prevent problems from surprising you. Balancing your checkbook is actually more than just keeping track of what check you wrote, when, and for how much. You need to give attention to how you are spending money, in all respects.

The good news is that there are as many methods of balancing your checkbook as there are people who spend money. A quick Internet search will turn up a variety of software products that will balance your checkbook, keep track of interest payments and due dates, and give you advice for managing your money. Some of these programs also work with tax software for people who file their own taxes. You can pick any of these products or keep a simple handwritten log of your accounts and spending.

Make sure to check your records against the statement provided by your bank. If there is a discrepancy between the two, call your bank right away and find out where the problem is. You may have forgotten to record a check or an ATM withdrawal, but it also may be that someone is using your bankcard without your knowledge. The same goes for credit cards.

Each time you balance your finances, take time to look at your remaining reserves. Do you have enough to last the rest of the semester or school year? If you continue spending at your current rate, how long will your funds last? You may find that you are spending well beyond your means and a correction is in order. This is your responsibility, but you are not alone. Your family can offer advice (and perhaps some extra cash) to help you adjust. Your local bank may have a financial advisor who can give you free advice. You should also approach your Resident Assistant (RA) about bringing a speaker to the floor to discuss personal finances. You are probably not the only one struggling to manage your money.

## Credit Reports

Any time you borrow money or use credit, your credit rating is affected. If you rent an apartment, your payment of utility bills shows on your credit report. Any time you take out a bank loan, such as for a car, or use a credit card, your credit rating could be affected. When you try to get new credit, such as securing a new credit card or getting a loan to purchase a car or house, the lender you are working with will check your credit rating. If you have consistently paid your bills on time, you will probably get the credit you are seeking and get good rates. However, the more problems you have on your report, such as missed payments or high balances, the more difficulty you will have getting credit.

This all serves as a caution to you. You want to get through college with as little debt as possible. When you do incur debt, you want to treat it carefully. It's not only your college education that could affect you for years to come. If you start to be concerned about your credit rating, you should seek assistance quickly. There are nonprofit agencies that can help you understand your credit report and give you some education at no cost. Your local bank or college bursar's office may have resources that you can use, and your parents are a good source of counsel as well. These are better options than those that charge fees for the same services.

## Chapter 4

#  So Much Stuff, So Little Space

So, you're leaving home and beginning a new life. It's time to pack everything you own and prepare to move it, right? Wrong. You are moving from an apartment or house to a single room—a single room you will likely share with someone else. You're moving from your previously permanent home to a place where you will live for only nine or ten months out of the year. Keeping this in mind, you should only take what you will need, will really use, and can transport back and forth several times over the next few years.

# Packing for a College Room

The first things you need to know are the size of your room and how many students will be sharing that space. Most students move into a residence hall room for their first semester of college, but if you are moving into a college suite or an apartment, you need to know how much space you have to yourself and how much you are sharing with others. Keep in mind that much of the floor space in your room will be filled by your bed, desk, and dresser. You have to think creatively and in three dimensions. What can be stacked, what can hang from the back of the door, and what can be stuffed in the back of your closet?

## QUESTION?

**What about furniture, such as a futon or lounge chair?**
It's a good idea to hold off on purchasing such items until you have lived in your college room for a while. Most residence halls are equipped with the essential pieces of furniture. If you do accumulate an extra chair or bookshelf, consider where you will store the furniture during the summer. Will you be able to use it again the following year, even if you change rooms?

The key to packing for a residence hall room is to take only those things you will need from the time you move in until the next time you visit home. You need to avoid unnecessary duplication of items as well. For example, don't bring two pairs of sneakers unless you will need them for different activities. Buying food in bulk may seem cost effective, but large bags and boxes will quickly eat up the space in your car and your residence hall room. One case of bottled water may store well under your bed, but several cases may take up too much valuable storage area. You may decide to make a list of things that your family can mail to you if you find you really need them. And remember: You can purchase many things once you get to college.

## *Toiletries and Medications*

Since you may be sharing a bathroom with everyone else on your floor, you need to be prepared to carry your toiletries to and from the bathroom each time you need to shower, brush your teeth, etc. The first thing you need is a bucket, basket, or some other kind of tote. Your best bet is something plastic; it can withstand getting wet and shampoo or other spills can be easily wiped off. You also want to get something that has openings on the sides or bottom to allow for water drainage. Finally, be sure to find something that is relatively small and has a handle. You only need to carry a few things for each trip to the shower, and something small will store unobtrusively in your room.

There are a few toiletries and accessories you should bring with you to college, but remember that you can restock at your college town's local grocery store and pharmacy as needed:

- Soap
- Soap dish, preferably covered
- Toothbrush
- Toothbrush case
- Toothpaste, dental floss, and mouthwash
- Hairbrush or comb
- Hair dryer, if you use one
- Shampoo and conditioner
- Cotton swabs
- Nail clippers and file
- Shaving cream and razors
- Deodorant
- Contact lens care equipment, if needed

Since everyone on your floor will be using the same set of showers you may want to get a pair of flip-flops or shower shoes. Your college bathroom will be cleaned regularly but many students still feel more comfortable keeping something between their feet and the tile floor of the shower. If you purchase shower shoes, get something open and durable. You will also need to remember to wash your shower shoes once in a while, as mildew and soap residue can build up over time.

Small or rural towns may not have stores with specialty products that you rely upon. If your college is in such an area and you generally use a very specific hair or skin care product, for example, make sure you bring an extra supply with you. You can always stock up when you go home for a break, but you don't want to run out in the meantime.

At some point in the first semester you are probably going to get sick. Whether it be a pesky cold or a twenty-four-hour flu, it is easy to catch something when so many people live and eat together in one place. So, come to college prepared with your own mini–medicine cabinet. You will want to be able to treat headaches, muscle aches, diarrhea, sinus congestion, and cold or flu symptoms whenever they occur. While your college health center may be able to treat all of these things, you will not want to wait for an appointment. And when you are feeling sick, a familiar remedy can be comforting and effective.

You also need to come with your own supplemental and prescription medications. You should pack any over-the-counter items, such as allergy pills or multivitamins. If you have prescriptions, you should get a couple of months' supply before heading to college and communicate with your campus health center about where you can go for refills. It's a good idea to leave a list of your medications with your family. They can always help you get refills or find the over-the-counter brand that you rely upon.

It is smart to pack a personal first aid kit as well. Some burn cream, antibiotic ointment, bandages, and a heating pad may serve you well during your first year at college. Some pharmacies and other stores carry premade first aid kits, or you can customize your own homemade kit.

## *Clothing*

You may want to look your best all of the time, but you also need to be practical about how much space you have in your room. How much dresser space will you have? Will you have a full closet to yourself, or will you have to share it with a roommate? How often will you have an occasion to wear that great dress? You need to think about these things before you can make final decisions about what to bring with you.

**ALERT!**

Don't buy new clothes and immediately pack them for college. Wash them once and wear them a little bit to make sure they are comfortable before heading to school. Your well-planned wardrobe will do you no good if you get to campus and find that a garment doesn't fit or it shrinks the first time you wash it.

Your initial clothing selection should get you from move-in day to your first trip home. Consider the climate where your school is located and pack accordingly. If you go to college in the northeast, you may want some sweaters but you can probably leave the winter coat for your second trip. When you go home for fall break or Thanksgiving, you can take home summer and fall clothing and bring back winter items, such as coats, hats, scarves, and gloves. However, if your college is in the south, you may not need any winter clothing until nearly December.

You know the basic clothing you will wear on a daily basis, but there is additional clothing you should remember as well:

- Bathing suit
- Bathrobe
- Exercise clothing
- Pajamas
- Rain jacket and umbrella
- Sports coat
- Nice dress

- Sweatpants
- Sweaters
- Ties

Clothing is a personal statement about who you are and what you're comfortable with. On large campuses you may find a wide range of clothing types among the students. On smaller campuses, where almost everyone might come from similar economic backgrounds, there may seem to be an unofficial uniform. When you visit campus, take note of what students are wearing; this may clue you into the climate there, and give you an idea of just how "dressed up" people get for class. However, your clothing should express your personality and make you comfortable. Don't spend excess energy trying to dress like everyone else. Fashion is fleeting, and regardless of your wardrobe, you'll become friends with the right people.

Also keep in mind that you will accumulate clothing while at college. You will likely purchase a sweatshirt with your college's name or logo on it. You will have dozens of opportunities to purchase or win T-shirts. Some groups, such as athletic teams and Greek organizations, have their own casual wear, such as shorts, hats, and shirts. And there will likely be a mall nearby with all your favorite stores—shopping is a favorite pastime among college students.

Very few colleges have an official dress code for students. This being the case, many students feel comfortable wearing sweatpants, shorts, and even pajamas around campus and to class. Dining hall etiquette is similarly relaxed and many students wear baseball caps during meals. The rule of thumb for students on campus is comfort.

A final note on clothing concerns the care you will give your clothes while at college. Even the most fastidious students find they do not have the time, energy, or desire to iron clothes on a regular basis. The same is true for dry cleaning. Even if you find a cheap dry cleaner adjacent to campus, you must choose between spending your money there or on social activities, such as late night pizza delivery. As you choose the clothes you will take to college, favor those that are wrinkle free or otherwise require little extra attention. Exclude items that cannot be thrown in the washer and dryer or hand-washed and hung up to dry in your room.

## Music, Movies, and Equipment

Throughout high school you have probably built a nice collection of music. It represents some of who you are and a lot of what you like. It also represents a good amount of money and a decent amount of space in your college room. You need to decide which music you will bring with you and which you will leave at home.

Think about the times you typically listen to music while you are at home. You will want music to exercise to, study to, and to have on in the background when you are just hanging out with your new friends. It's a good idea to have a variety of types of music, as much to serve your various moods as to show your roommate and new friends what you enjoy. Keep in mind that your roommate will be doing the same thing and the two of you will have to compromise on the music that is played when you are in the room.

Online swapping of music and movies has become very popular among college students. The recording industry has made efforts to curb illegal sharing of copyrighted material, including filing lawsuits against students on college campuses. Some students have been shut out of campus networks for using too much bandwidth. Therefore, use file-swapping services at your own risk and with caution.

Unless you're going to work as a DJ while at college, try to narrow your collection down to one small box, perhaps the size of a shoebox. Then pull four or five CDs out of the box. You will get new CDs at college by attending concerts, from friends, or just purchasing new releases. You can always bring more back with you when you return from your first trip home.

Movie collections are a little different from music collections. Like music, they represent a lot about you and are a good icebreaker with new friends. However, getting together in someone's room to watch movies is a college staple these days. When there is nothing else to do on campus (other than the dozen or so activities sponsored by the college), you can always get a group together to watch a movie.

**QUESTION?**

**What about using a computer as a DVD player and/or stereo?**
If your computer is a laptop this is a good idea, allowing you to take your entertainment anywhere in your residence hall or on trips to and from home. A desktop computer with these functions is less flexible and not really an alternative to a television in your room.

Keep in mind that each generation has a few staples in its movie collection. If all your friends from high school own a particular movie, your new friends at college will probably have it too. Leave those movies at home. You also want to leave behind any home movies you have, such as family vacations and birthdays. However, if you have your high school graduation recorded, you may want to bring that for those times when you're feeling nostalgic. Definitely bring your favorite movies and any complete series that you own. And don't hesitate to bring movies that you feel are a little childish. The movie you adore from your childhood is likely a favorite of others as well and can be the starting point for a great friendship.

Although residence hall lounges are still equipped with televisions, and sometimes DVD/VHS players, most students bring their own to college. If you're going to bring your television to college (and have coordinated it with your new roommate), be certain that you really have space for it. You want something that can be easily moved to and from college, as well as around your room each time you rearrange your furniture. Remember that your TV may get damaged while you're at college, so a very significant investment is not a good idea for your college room. You do want a set that is cable-ready and has a remote control. You probably won't have space for an entertainment center, but a small cart or stand that will also accommodate your DVD/VHS player is a good idea.

Since residence hall rooms are small, you do not need a surround sound system. Such a system may be cool, but your TV or stereo alone will be loud enough to annoy your neighbors. If your stereo system is a portable unit, you're in good shape. If you have several components, you again need to think about space. You are likely going to place your components on your desk, on a shelf, or on top of your dresser. The fewer components you bring, the better for your space limitations. Large speakers will have to find floor space but need to be placed so that people don't trip over the wires or bump into the speakers.

## A Touch of Home

It is important to make your residence hall room feel a little bit like home. You will be sleeping, eating, studying, hanging out, and talking with family and friends on the phone all in this one room. You need to be comfortable here and make your guests feel comfortable as well.

Posters have long been a staple for college students. If you have some favorites, bring them along. If not, your college bookstore is certain to have some on hand. You will also learn from the bookstore or housing office how best to affix posters to your walls; housing officials frown on punching holes in walls and some kinds of tape will remove the paint or stain the wall. Keep in mind that posters cover a large section of wall and make a statement about you. Only display posters you don't mind friends and family seeing.

**ALERT!**

Many colleges have restrictions on the use of tapestries. Few schools allow you to hang things from your ceiling and none permit you to block smoke detectors and other safety equipment. Tapestries remain a popular wall covering with college students, but you should review your college's policies before draping your entire room in tapestries.

Many students bring photos of family, friends, and occasions, such as high school graduation. You will want a few framed photographs for your desk. You may be able to hang framed photos on your walls, but getting the frames to stick without damaging the wall may be difficult, depending on the construction of your building. Most students create a collage of photos around the desk or bed, adding to the collage as they take pictures of their college experiences. These collages can be a comfort to you and a great conversation starter with your new friends.

You will also want to bring some keepsakes with you, but choose them carefully. The things you bring are likely to experience some wear and tear; they may be examined by visitors to your room, and at worst, may be lost or stolen. An antique snow globe from your grandmother is probably best left at home. Your high school yearbook, an album of pictures, and a favorite mug are small items that can help you feel connected to home.

You will want to think before bringing special collections. Stuffed animals, for example, provide good decoration for a room and don't weigh much. A collection of trading cards or old coins, on the other hand, may prove to be a waste of space and not get much use while at college. But if you have a book collection that might be helpful in your classes, you may want to bring it, despite the space it will require. Think about how you will use your collection before adding it to the growing list of things to bring.

## Bringing It Back Again

Loading your belongings into the car and heading to college for the first time will be exciting and fun. At some point, however, you are going to have to pack all of it back in the car and get it home again. In the interim months you will have accumulated new books, clothing, and other items. For this reason, it is important to leave some room in your car the first time around.

Sometime in midsemester, you should identify the items you are not going to use for the rest of the year and ship them home. If family or friends come to visit, send some things back with them. If you head home for spring break or take a weekend trip with your new friends to show them where you grew up, take some things home and leave them there.

Many students don't begin packing their rooms until exams are finished, and many parents are frustrated when they arrive and find a room that is completely unpacked. In addition to taking things home throughout the semester use study breaks during finals week to pack items you don't need anymore. The more you have done before your family arrives the better.

You may find that many of the things in your room won't be needed again until you return to college for your second year. Why take them home just to leave them in boxes? Inquire with your housing office about storage companies in the area around your college. Most schools cannot provide storage space but will know where students can rent a storage locker for the summer. To be most effective, rent a locker with several friends, splitting the cost and adding help with moving heavy items. Just be careful that you don't store too much—when you graduate you will have to move it all home, put it up for sale, or donate it.

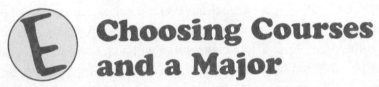

**Chapter 5**

# Choosing Courses and a Major

Your primary purpose for going to college is to get an education. You may want that education to increase your knowledge, increase your earning potential, or help you serve others. In addition to your formal education you will learn how to apply knowledge, gain interpersonal skills, and have a tremendous amount of fun. But your central mission is earning a degree, and this is accomplished by completing academic requirements. At college, you alone must ensure that you are taking the proper courses to achieve your goals.

## *Advisement*

Sometime in the summer, you should be assigned an academic advisor. This may be a professor who will be teaching a required first-year student course, a randomly selected professor, or a member of the academic advising staff. Your advisor is your personal expert on academic matters and should be the first person with whom you consult about course selections. She will be able to give you an idea of which classes new students typically select, some suggestions about classes that will fill requirements or help you explore possible majors, and explain the class registration process. Your advisor will also help you with dates and procedures for dropping or adding classes to your schedule.

At some schools, you will register for classes after you arrive on campus and meet with your academic advisor. At other schools, you will register for classes prior to stepping foot on campus. If you fall into the latter category, you must be more assertive about getting the advice you will need to pick appropriate classes.

Another good source of advice is other students. If you know students who are already attending your college, get in touch with them and ask for suggestions about classes you should take. Keep in mind that their advice will be coming from a much different perspective. They can tell you which professors are approachable, which buildings are close to your residence hall, and what class combinations were overwhelming for other first year students. If you don't know a student currently at your college, call the orientation office and ask to speak with a student, or call the admissions office and ask to speak with one of the student tour guides. These students may be less candid than someone you already know, but they can still offer a good perspective.

If you truly believe you know what you want to do after college, ask a professional in that field what she would recommend. For example, if you want to be a dentist, ask your dentist what she would take if she were starting college again. In addition to possibly gaining some good advice, you're developing a deeper relationship with a person who might be able to give you an internship, summer job, or job recommendation in that field.

Part of getting good advice is asking good questions. Think about what you want to accomplish during your college education. For example, if you want to study in Italy for a year, you may be best served by beginning Italian classes as soon as possible. The people you are seeking advice from can help you with this type of planning, and they can best help you if you first form an idea of your goals and then ask good questions.

## *A Balanced Schedule*

The list of course offerings you initially receive will include a wide range of classes. Even after you have solicited advice from informed people, and received unsolicited advice from interested relatives and friends, you'll have a number of courses in mind. Some classes are safe bets because you took something similar in high school. If you had two years of Spanish in high school, then taking the introductory Spanish class at college is a safe bet. The college course will still be challenging because it will move at a faster pace and your professor will expect more of you, but your familiarity with the topic will serve you well. However, if the high school and college courses are too similar, you may receive a duplicate experience, and thus waste your time and money. For this reason, it's a good idea to speak with the professor before registering for his class.

## QUESTION?

**Do you have to take foreign language classes in college, even if you took them in high school?**
Every school has a unique policy on foreign languages. Many schools require you to have taken at least one year of language courses at the college level. Other schools will acknowledge your high school language achievements as sufficient. Some colleges also offer a proficiency exam that gives you a reprieve from taking language classes if you pass it.

Other classes might be interesting, but fall completely outside of your academic experience thus far. Astronomy is a fascinating course that might fill a general requirement, but if you've never taken a similar class, the new material could give you trouble. If there is no prerequisite—a course you must pass before you can take a higher-level course—then the college feels that you are eligible for the class. Don't be afraid to try something new.

Early in your undergraduate career you have the opportunity to be creative with the classes you take. If you are intent on majoring in biology then you might select a course in pottery or dance as an elective. You will have the opportunity to think in new ways, meet a different group of students, and gain a better-rounded education by experimenting in this way. You will also gain an appreciation for the type of work other disciplines do and a vocabulary that will help you communicate with a wider variety of people. As your college career progresses you will have less and less opportunity to take classes outside of your major—do so while you can. Whatever you choose to do, the basic goal is to have a balanced schedule. Pick a few classes that fall within your comfort zone, and pick at least one that represents a challenge or a creative opportunity.

New students often get nervous about the academic demands of college. It will be harder, faster, and more demanding than high school. But remember that your college admitted you because they expect you to succeed. Your application showed something about you that they chose to believe in. If experienced professionals believe in you, you have a good reason to believe in yourself.

## Personal Patterns and Preferences

Are you a morning person or a night owl? Do you enjoy solitary or group work? While your answers to such questions will change while you're at college, you should have an idea of what time of day you have the most energy, when you do your best thinking, and how you prefer to work. When selecting classes try to pick sections that are available when you are naturally most alert. Unfortunately, as a new student, you will likely have to choose from the sections upper-class students don't want, so you may end up with a class or two at 8:00 A.M. If this happens, and you are not a morning person, you will have to make the best of things by getting a good night's sleep before your class and using your alert time to do your studying. While course descriptions rarely tell you if there will be lots of group work, you can usually tell if there will be a lot of reading—an indication of the kind of work the professor will expect in class.

If you have not yet declared a major and do not have a course load defined for you, experiment by taking a variety of classes. It's also important to know what motivates and excites you. If you do not enjoy reading, then history, literature, and other humanities courses may only cause you stress. If you enjoy hands-on learning, then science lab courses might be a good choice, or political science courses, if you are looking for active debates.

Even if you have a major or course load in mind, it's important to diversify your education. Just because you have a talent or interest in a particular area does not mean you should overload your schedule with classes that deal only with that topic. Keeping a variety of classes in your schedule helps give you a better-rounded education and increases your ability in areas where you are not as strong. Always schedule one or two classes that play to your strengths, but balance them out with a few new interests.

## Core Requirements

Once you declare a major, there will be a particular set of courses you must complete. Similarly, you may have a set of basic classes, or core requirements, which you must complete in order to earn a degree from your college. Often you can fill a particular requirement by choosing one course from a list within a particular category. For example, in order to complete a cultural understanding requirement you may be able to choose from several history courses. You can find information about core requirements in your college bulletin.

You'll have to make a decision about when to complete your core requirements. One strategy is to complete all core requirements as soon as possible in your college career, leaving your final years to focus on courses in your major. Another approach is to do things in the completely opposite order, focusing on your major initially and completing core requirements in your final semesters of college. For most students, the sensible choice rests somewhere in the middle. Taking one or two core requirement courses each semester keeps you on track for graduation and allows you to take other courses for your major, minor, or personal interest. It's also nice to have one or two less challenging classes while you're taking the toughest courses in your major. As a senior, you may not be overwhelmed by an introductory course, even if the freshmen in your class are.

**FACT**

Your college bulletin often represents your academic contract with the college. The requirements and expectations listed there will apply to you until you earn your degree. Although a new bulletin will be published every year or two you need to hold on to your original bulletin. It can help you track your progress toward your degree.

## When and How to Declare a Major

You may have come to college with a career goal in mind. Or you may know that you will need a college education but are not certain about a major or career. Unless you plan to be involved in a specific preprofessional program, such as premedical, then you have some time before you need to declare a major. Your first semesters at college should be spent taking courses in a variety of areas, filling some core requirements, and allowing your interests to develop.

Most schools will require you to declare a major as late as the end of your second year or the beginning of your third year. If you're uncertain about what your major should be, visit your career center and begin to explore your options. Career centers offer a variety of resources to help students sift through interests, aspirations, possible majors, and potential careers. They can also help you understand how a single major can launch a career in one of several fields, giving you more flexibility and perhaps peace of mind when you declare a major.

When you know what your major will be, or at least your *first* major since you will be able to change your mind, sit down with your academic advisor and discuss your plans. Your registrar will have the official major declaration form to complete. You will need to select an advisor for your new major. If you have one in mind, approach her and ask if she is willing to be your major advisor. She'll likely ask you why you want to major in that field and why you want her as an advisor. For the latter question, you might talk about how you have enjoyed previous courses you have had with her, feedback from other students who are majors in that subject, or lectures and publications for which the professor is known. Choose a major advisor carefully—this person will advise you on courses, help position you for graduate school or a job after college, and will likely write you a letter of recommendation upon graduation. If your desired major advisor is unavailable, perhaps due to a sabbatical (leave from teaching in order to pursue research) or an already full load of advisees, ask her whom she would recommend as an advisor in this particular major.

It's important to choose a major that interests you, but it should also lead you to a career or graduate program once you graduate. If you only have a general idea of a career you might enjoy, declare a less specific major, like business or communications. This will prepare you for a wide array of jobs and still allow you to further shape your education in graduate school.

Many majors will have an associated club or interest group. Many times you will be a member of this organization by virtue of being a major in the field. Your initial impression may be one of disdain. How much fun can, for example, the history club really be? In fact these organizations are valuable to you during your time at college and perhaps beyond. The group consists of students who share at least one of your interests and will have the attention of faculty in the department. You will have a built-in resource for forming study groups as well as learning about professors and classes you hope to take. These clubs will also sponsor speakers or take trips that might help you further define what you want to do with your life. Finally, your participation in club activities might help connect you with alumni or professionals in your field who can help you network to get an internship or a job after college.

## Minors and Dual Majors

Most colleges offer you the opportunity to declare a minor area of study, and some actually require such a declaration. The idea is that you can develop a concentration of knowledge on a particular subject, in addition to your major area of study. Many students who declare minors try to pick something that compliments the major they have chosen. An education major, for example, may choose a history minor to help prepare him for a career teaching social studies. Other students choose a minor that seems completely unrelated to their major; a chemistry major may choose an English minor to help improve his writing ability. Unless you're involved in a specific preprofessional program, such a premedical or preveterinary, you are best served by choosing a minor in an area of personal interest. The more you enjoy the learning process, the more you will gain from it.

**FACT**

Your minor will show up on your college transcript, and perhaps your first resume, but after that it is of little interest to potential employers. So, treat your minor as a chance to explore a subject you really enjoy. Try biology or art even if your major is political science. You may discover a lifelong pursuit outside your career.

Many schools also give students the opportunity to declare two simultaneous majors. Termed a double or dual major, this choice allows a student to become an expert in two areas of study. Many students choose complementary majors, such as history and political science. There is some debate about whether there is a real advantage to having two majors. However, students who declare two majors have to be that much more focused and organized in their course selections. Such students must look at courses offered several semesters in advance to plan the order in which they take classes.

In the case of minors and dual majors, it's always a good idea to speak with your academic advisor about your interests and plans. You'll want as much help as possible ensuring that you are completing your major and minor requirements as efficiently as possible, keeping up with core requirements, and preparing yourself for a job or graduate school after college. Additionally, consider a visit to the career center. Present the staff there with your ultimate post-college plans and ask for their thoughts about an appropriate major and/or minor.

## *Study Abroad Opportunities*

While you are a college student, you can take advantage of the opportunity to visit, study in, and perhaps even live in other parts of the world. Study in another country or away from your home campus is referred to as study abroad, and it sometimes includes programs on another domestic campus. There are programs that will allow you to study the language or culture of another country, and programs that help you study your major from the perspective of another environment. Students who study abroad report significant changes in themselves. They see the world differently, have a new understanding of what can be done with a particular major, and often develop a new sense of self. Though going abroad can be scary, it can also enrich your life in ways you never thought possible.

**ALERT!**

When planning a trip to study abroad, be certain to visit your financial aid office. Your aid package may not be acceptable to some programs, and if you are going abroad without aid, you need to ensure that your assistance package will still be available when you return. Be sure to speak with your financial aid officer early in the planning process.

Many colleges have their own study abroad programs or have agreements with colleges that have such programs. Often there is an office for this type of study, or at least a primary contact person who coordinates plans for students who want to study abroad. One advantage of using a program sponsored or approved by your campus is that your school has already accredited the classes you will take while abroad. That is, the classes you take away from your campus will transfer back and count toward your degree and graduation requirements. Another advantage is that your financial aid package will be least affected by working through a school-sponsored program.

You may find that your school does not offer a program that has what you're looking for. There may be another school that does offer the program you are seeking, or you could try to arrange a study abroad experience on your own. In these cases, you need to work closely with your academic advisor and campus study abroad coordinator. You will have to find out details from the sponsoring school so that your college can accept the courses and continue to keep you listed as an active student. In some cases, you may need to temporarily withdraw or take a leave of absence from your college. If that happens, you need to ask how to re-enroll, how the absence will affect your graduation requirements, and how your financial aid package will change. It is worth the effort if you can choose the program that best meets your interests and goals, but be prepared to work a little harder to get what you want.

## Semester and Year Programs

While there are several other options, the majority of students choose to study abroad for the term of one semester or one academic year. In both cases, you get the opportunity to live in another place and reach beyond the tourist mentality. In addition to your academic work you will gain a better understanding of another culture, get a new perspective of your own culture, and perhaps make some lasting friendships. It will help if you are proficient in the language of your host country. If you are not skilled in the language, you should at least be capable enough to understand simple written and verbal communication.

An often overlooked advantage of studying abroad for an extended period is the opportunity to play host to family and friends. Spring break on your home campus, for example, may give your friends a chance to come and visit you, experience a new place, and catch you up on everything going on back at school. Your parents or other family members might like the vacation as well. No matter how much you are enjoying your time abroad it is always good to see familiar faces and hear your native language.

If you're going to be in one country for an academic year, you may also be able to take advantage of other opportunities that will be helpful to you later in life. For instance, you could find an internship. Whether this is for credit or not, you will gain powerful experience and have an item on your resume that will set you apart from many other students. You may also be able to tutor local students in your native language or find a community service opportunity to become involved with. Look beyond the tourist activities and think creatively about how you can maximize your time abroad.

Most study abroad programs will either house you at a university, set you up with an apartment, or arrange for you to stay with a local family. In any case, you will quickly learn the native language and adapt to local customs, if you take full advantage of the opportunity. Though most students find a new culture to be intimidating at first, immersing yourself in the experience will prove to be very rewarding in the end.

## Summer and Intersession Programs

If you cannot leave campus for an academic year or even a full semester, ask your campus study abroad coordinator about summer opportunities. There are a variety of programs lasting from five to eight weeks in the summer that can give you a solid experience in another country. Many times these programs occur through a course offered on your campus and may involve traveling to several countries. Summer programs still offer you the chance to learn about another country, its culture, and its people. Shorter programs may allow you to have the best of both worlds—study abroad for academic credit and a summer job to pay for the experience.

An increasing number of schools are also developing study abroad programs for intersession or break periods. January is often an opportunity for faculty to take a group of students to another country for a few weeks. This trip is typically done in the context of a particular class, but is usually available to students regardless of their declared major. Sometimes these classes will be interdisciplinary, giving a few professors the opportunity to collaborate on a course in which the students may think broadly about the location and the subject matter. A significant advantage for many students is that January trips abroad often involve heading to a warmer place. Spending three weeks of January in Mexico, for example, may be a more attractive option than staying on campus in New England.

## Chapter 6

# Traveling to and from Campus

Your first drive to college will be an exciting one, but before long, you'll get to know that route like the back of your hand. You will probably make the trip to and from college between eight and twenty-five times during your college career, so you should consider that journey and everything that comes with it. Whether you are traveling alone or with friends, in your vehicle or by public transportation, there are a variety of things to keep in mind.

**ALERT!**

Some schools restrict car privileges for first-year students. You may be prohibited from having a car on campus or restricted to parking in a remote lot. Failure to follow college car policies may result in loss of future car privileges or other disciplinary action. Learn your school's policy before deciding to bring your car to campus.

## Your Car, Your Responsibility

The seemingly simple decision to bring your car to campus carries with it several details that need your attention. One of the first will be where to park. Larger schools sometimes have an entire office devoted to parking regulation. At smaller schools, security offices usually manage this function. Get in touch with this office and learn how to register your vehicle, where you may park on campus, and if there are other policies that apply to you as a driver. Be prepared to pay for parking privileges, particularly at larger schools.

You may decide to flaunt authority and bring your car to campus without registering it with your school. In fact, some students do this quite successfully. However, if you're going to park your car on city streets or in residential neighborhoods you must recognize that you have given up the advantages of campus parking. You may have to walk further to get to your vehicle, your vehicle will not be in a patrolled lot, and neighbors may become unfriendly if you park in the space immediately in front of their house. Cities also have schedules for street cleaning and snow removal, so you must move your car on those designated days or risk accruing tickets.

Of course, you can't drive your car without being properly insured. Check with your insurance agent to see if your current coverage will be sufficient in your college's state. You will also want to ask your agent about discounts for college students, maintaining good grades, or keeping a safe driving record. You (or your family) already know how expensive car insurance is, so any amount you can save is well worth it.

Once you are on campus with your car you have to make some hard decisions. You may be one of the few new students with a car, and as such may be bombarded with requests for a quick ride to the store, mall, or local fast food restaurant. Sadly, some people will befriend you only because you have a car. While this may help you meet people initially, the friends who value you only for your ability to be a chauffeur will not be the friends that endure throughout your college career. You will also have to explain why you say "yes" to some people and "no" to others.

Car theft is a real concern in some cities, and car alarms are a real annoyance in many neighborhoods. If you park where you cannot hear your car alarm disable it and find another way to secure your car. Also be sure not to leave CDs, cell phones, or other petty theft targets sitting in plain view in your car.

Prior to arriving on campus, make a decision about how you will use your car. Is it just for trips home, only for weekend trips to the mall or movies, or for no more than one trip per day? Think about how you will respond to requests to take your new friends out for a quick errand. You may want to decide how many miles a week is reasonable. Keep track of how much you're driving and be certain that it isn't taking away from time you should be studying or could be socializing in other ways.

Before long, some of your friends will ask to borrow your car, usually just for a "quick trip" to get some take-out or pick up a few things. Lending your car to others is very risky. Are they good drivers? Do they even have driver's licenses? What if they get pulled over by the police or break some local laws while driving your car? Will they clean your car if they spill food or drinks in it? What if they get in a serious accident while driving your car? There are too many things that can go wrong when lending your car to friends, so plan to be the sole operator while you are at college.

Either prior to heading to campus or soon after your arrival, you should find a mechanic. While you're at college, you are likely to need an oil change and attention for things such as belts, brakes, and filters. You'll want to locate a mechanic you can trust. There may be a car dealership or a major service chain near your campus, but your best bet is probably a local mechanic who treats students well. Ask your RA, academic advisor, or even a department secretary about good mechanics near the school.

**How do you say "no" to friends who want to borrow your car?**
The best thing to say is that you simply aren't comfortable with others driving your car. You can also say that you promised your family that no one else would drive the car but you. Whatever method you choose, saying "no" will help protect you and your car.

It's a good idea to take your car in for a tune-up prior to taking a long trip. You should always be certain that your brakes and tires are in good shape. If you decide to do this yourself, be sure to check your tire pressure as well as oil and other fluid levels. It's a good idea to have a current atlas and a flashlight in the car as well.

## Ride Boards

Many colleges maintain ride boards so students without cars can find rides home and those with cars can have company on a long drive. Recently, schools have begun to host such resources on electronic bulletin boards. Find out where your school's ride board is well in advance of needing a ride or an extra passenger for a trip.

If you're posting a request on a ride board, try to be general about your destination. For example, rather than say that you are trying to reach the 1600 block of Elm Street, advertise that you are looking for a ride to the greater Lawton area. Once you have connected with a driver, see how close to home she is able to get you. You may also want to advertise the time that you are hoping to depart from campus or arrive in your hometown area.

Before accepting a ride with someone from a ride board, it's a good idea to meet and get to know each other. You'll want to ask who else will be taking the trip with you and get a feel for the driver's general personality. Find out what stops the driver plans to make, the route he is planning to follow, and his timetable for making the trip. You also want to ask about space for your baggage—how much are you able to bring with you on this trip? Trust your instincts; if you do not feel comfortable with this driver for any reason, seek another ride.

If you are a passenger in a carpool, you should always offer to help pay for gas on the trip. You also want to ask permission before eating or drinking in another person's car. If you are the only passenger, you should refrain from using headphones, at least at the start of the trip, so your driver doesn't feel like a chauffeur.

You and the others sharing a ride need to talk about whether this is a one-way or round trip. If you will be returning with this same person, you need to exchange home and cell phone numbers, have a set time and place to meet for the return trip, and be clear about how much stuff you can bring back to campus. For example, if you are returning to campus in January, is there enough space in the car for your skis or an extra suitcase? You also want to have some idea of other rides near your area. If your driver cancels for the return trip, who else can you call for a ride back to school?

## *Airlines*

Airline travel has the advantage of being quick and easy to navigate. Even the additional time needed for security checks and making connections often outweighs the disadvantages of driving. If you fly to and from college frequently, register for a frequent flyer program and accrue miles that you can exchange for free travel later on. In addition, you will find that airlines sometimes engage in price wars, each offering you a lower price for your particular flight. This can add affordability to the benefits of travel by plane. Usually, the sooner you book your flight, the better price you are able to secure.

There are additional security measures involved with air travel, so plan your trip accordingly. Wear clothing and shoes with little or no metal. Check your pockets and carry-on bags carefully for prohibited items such as pocketknives, pepper spray, and scissors. If you are bringing gifts home do not wrap them prior to your flight. Get to the airport at least an hour before your flight is scheduled to depart. And be prepared to be patient, especially during peak travel periods.

If you have a flexible schedule and are traveling during a busy season, inquire with your airline about overbooked flights. You can tell the ticket agent that you are willing to be bumped if the airline needs an extra seat. Airlines will usually give you extra frequent flyer miles or some other payment for missing your flight. You may also be able to get a meal voucher from the airline to eat in one of the airport restaurants while you pass the time.

**ALERT!**

You can often save money by booking flights in advance, and you can reference the academic calendar ahead of time to know when break periods occur. However, you'll also need to coordinate your flight date and time with your residence hall's closing schedule. If your residence hall closes for break at 10:00 A.M. on a Friday but your flight isn't until Saturday morning, you will need to make other arrangements for that night.

Everyone has heard stories about airlines losing luggage or shipping it to the wrong destination. Be certain you know exactly what you packed in your luggage, keeping a list of those items in your carry-on bag, if possible. Be sure that your luggage has tags that include your name and address, and keep your claim check in your purse or wallet. If your checked luggage is lost, the staff at the baggage claim desk can give you an estimate of when it will arrive. You can insist that the airline deliver your luggage to your final destination, and they will do so free of charge.

It's all well and good to have your trip home planned, but how will you get to the airport? In larger cities you will probably have to take a bus, train, or cab, if you can't find a ride with a friend. Colleges without easy access to such mass transit will likely run a shuttle service during peak travel periods on campus. You usually need to sign up in advance for this service and may have to wait at the airport for several hours before your scheduled departure.

Such shuttle services may also charge a nominal fee and have limited space for baggage. Check on shuttle services well in advance of your actual travel. When signing up for a shuttle have all of your travel information with you, including airline, flight numbers, and time of departure or arrival.

When traveling by plane, be prepared for long lines and delays. Pack your carry-on with a book to read for fun, some schoolwork you need to do over break, a couple of magazines, or some music to listen to. Make sure that your cell phone is fully charged before you leave so that you can spend time in the airport calling friends or family.

## Trains and Buses

Years ago, trains and buses were the preferred method of getting to and from college. While they have recently fallen out of vogue, trains and buses are affordable and underrated modes of travel. In addition to potentially saving money you will have fewer lines to wait in and more time to study, read a book for fun, or write holiday cards during the trip.

Train travel has become easier through use of the Internet. You can plan your entire trip, including stops in multiple cities, as well as purchase your train tickets without ever leaving home. Train travel has the advantage of snack cars or meal service, and the newer cars sometimes offer plugs for laptop computers. You are also able to get up and move around on trains, which makes the trip more comfortable.

Train stations and bus stops are often located in dismal or obscure parts of cities. For this reason, it's important that you plan to have someone pick you up as soon as you arrive at the station or stop. If you have a cell phone, keep the battery charged while you are traveling so you can call a family member or friend once you've reached the train or bus terminal.

Bus travel is also relatively easy and may get you closer to your home than a train, airplane, or car ride from a college friend. In addition, bus travel tends to be much cheaper than other modes. However, buses often restrict your options of when you travel, and are lacking in amenities and space. If you take a long bus trip to or from college it's important to get out and stretch during stops, even if it means interrupting a good nap. Check with your campus or conduct a quick Internet search to learn which bus companies are convenient for your location.

## Academic and Holiday Calendars

Before you leave for college, you should have an idea of the calendar for the academic year. Your registrar or housing office will send you information about school holidays and when residence halls are closed. Pay careful attention to these dates. You need to plan your travel so you can depart before buildings close and return after official opening times.

**QUESTION?**

**What if you can't go home for a break?**
If you can't go home for a break, see if one of your friends will take you home with her. Conversely, if one of the other students on your floor needs a place to go, consider bringing her home with you. Sharing break with a friend is usually preferable to staying in the residence hall.

There are times when your school will be closed but residence halls will remain open, and others when the entire campus will shut down. If travel is prohibitive due to cost, your academic workload, or family travel conflicts you might consider staying in the residence hall for a break period. Be warned that this is a lonely time on campus. However, you can use the time to catch up on your course work, rent movies from a local video store, or just relax. This is always a good time to catch up on your sleep or further explore the area around your campus.

It is also wise to consider national holiday travel patterns. For example, since the day before Thanksgiving is a big travel day, you might plan your travel for a day or two earlier. If you are unable to avoid high traffic times, be prepared to wait in lines and be patient. Bring a good book or a portable CD player to help you pass the time.

## *Staying Late on Campus*

Although your residence hall may be open during a break period, your housing office will almost certainly want to know if you are remaining on campus. As with any good bureaucracy, they probably have a form you need to fill out in order to officially remain on campus. Staying on campus for a break will rarely cost you any extra money, so filling out the form is a good idea. In addition to staying on the housing staff's good side, you will remain undisturbed by facilities, housekeeping, and security staff. While on campus during a break, be extra vigilant about security. Be sure that your room door is locked when you are asleep or out of the room, and watch for unfamiliar people around the campus.

**ALERT!**

If you plan to spend a break period on campus, be sure to use extra caution. Many predators see college breaks as opportunities to assault, mug, or otherwise take advantage of isolated students. To help protect yourself, always keep your cell phone charged, avoid walking alone at night, and keep all valuables safely stowed in your locked residence hall room.

You may find that you are unable to leave campus for a break by the designated time. If this is the case, you need to speak with your RA as soon as possible about how to stay late or what other options are available for you. During winter break, for example, many housing offices do a room-to-room check to make sure that windows are secure, appliances are unplugged, and residents have gone home. A few hours may not make a difference, but an extra day or two could be problematic for you and your school. If you are not able to stay in your room beyond the closing time, you might consider waiting for your ride at a local mall or getting a hotel room for the extra night.

If you are able to remain on campus during a break, you need to find out what services will remain open. Often libraries, cafeterias, and athletic facilities shut down so staffs can enjoy the holiday with family. If the dining hall is no longer open, you'll need to set a budget for meals. And if you are planning to get ahead on your work, you need to know when you can get into the library or computer lab. It's also important to know who to call if problems occur. For example, if a pipe breaks in your bathroom, who can you call to repair it if all the school offices are closed? Typically your security office will be staffed during break, but check with your RA about such things before she leaves for her own break.

Another thing to do if you are on campus for a break period is find out who else will be staying in your building. Take this opportunity to get to know some new people—have a few meals together or go out to catch a movie. Even if you don't become best friends with these other students, at least you'll have some company during your break on campus.

You can also find other opportunities for some company on campus during a break. Perhaps a professor will invite you to her house for a meal, or you and the international students who can't travel home will get together to see a movie at some point. If you have developed a good relationship with your custodian he may bring you a homecooked meal during the break, or a commuter student that you have a class with may invite you out with some of her friends. Look for opportunities to be social during this time. Though it's important for you to get ahead in your studies, small social events will keep you from getting too bored or lonely.

Remaining on campus during a break period also gives you the chance to earn some extra money. Perhaps one of your professors is going to need a babysitter for a few days around the holidays. Or, maybe the local pizza place will need some extra help since all the regular student employees will be out of town. To make sure you avail yourself of all possible opportunities, do your best to make these arrangements well in advance of the break.

**Chapter 7**

# Establishing Residence in a New Place

As you are probably beginning to realize, the transition to college is a complex process. Who knew there were so many details related to that single decision? Just establishing yourself in a new place is full of small and large decisions you must make, each very important. However, you will likely establish residence in several new places throughout your life, and the skills you learn during your move to college will serve you well in the future.

## *Residence Halls*

Most students choose or are required to live on campus when they first head to college, and this means living in a residence hall. Colleges, specifically housing offices, are becoming more particular about how they refer to living spaces on campus. For many, a dormitory is just a place to sleep, store your personal effects, and occasionally study while you go about the business of completing your degree. A residence hall, on the other hand, is an active place where curricular, cocurricular, and extracurricular learning takes place. Most housing offices tout their residence halls as vibrant communities where students will feel at home and develop meaningful friendships while pursuing a college education. They aren't just "dorms" anymore.

Before your family leaves, make sure that you have everything you need. Once the car is unpacked, you can go to a local store to pick up items that were too bulky to bring, such as a lamp or pillow. Once your family heads back home, you may not have the opportunity to run such errands for a while.

In Chapter 2, you read about filling out your housing survey and possibly requesting a specific residence hall. When you actually get on campus and move into your room, you need to do a few things before unpacking. First, inspect the details of the room. Try the phone, test the desk and dresser drawers, open windows and closets, check both sides of your mattress for tears, and search the walls for damage. While the college will work hard to correct these issues before you get to campus, it's possible that some problems may slip through the cracks. If your RA has not provided you with a room condition form, make your own and note any damage that exists before you unpack. Communicate these concerns to your RA and keep your list so that you are not held accountable for the damage when you move out of your room at the end of the school year.

As you and your family unpack your belongings, don't worry too much about getting things set up just right. You and your roommate will likely rearrange the room at least once in the first month of school. You do want to get clothes put away, hang a few things on the walls, and store suitcases or boxes that you are not sending back with your family. If you have a refrigerator, make sure it is located near an outlet and plugged in. Similarly, your electronics will need to be near the appropriate outlets. Your television must be near the cable outlet and your computer near the network connection.

After you have things generally unpacked, connect your computer and make sure that nothing was damaged during the trip to campus. If you're having difficulty connecting to the campus network, talk to your RA about how to get help. Some problems are common enough that your RA can give you a quick answer. Others will require computer services staff to come look at your equipment.

After you've met your roommate and mostly set up your room, walk around the building and get the lay of the land. Learn where the lounges are, if there's a kitchen in the building, and where laundry and vending services are located. If you still have time before orientation activities begin, take a quick tour of the campus with your roommate. This will give you a sense of where your residence hall is in relation to classes, the cafeteria, the library, and other places you will visit often in your new life.

**ALERT!**

Some students will have the option to live at home and commute to college. From a cost perspective, this is usually a very good idea. However, commuting students must work hard to become part of campus life and benefit from the experience beyond the classroom. If you commute, find good places on campus to study and join several college organizations to help you meet more people.

## *Apartments*

Renting your own apartment when you get to college, if this is even an option at your school, will provide you with more independence and more responsibility. There are numerous details to tend to and no office or advisor to help you keep on top of your commitments. Many students believe that it will be cheaper to live off campus, but most find that an apartment is more expensive in the end. Some students enjoy the distance from the bustle of campus, and many students are actually able to save some money by living in an apartment.

If you're going to get an apartment off campus, begin searching for a place as soon as you have finalized your college choice. You will likely be one of hundreds of students looking for an apartment, so the earlier you begin the better options you will have. Your college housing office may have some resources for locating off-campus apartments. If not, look through a local newspaper or work with a realtor to identify possibilities. You need to consider frequency and amount of rent costs, costs of utilities not included with rent, safety, and proximity to campus and public transportation. And you should always try to visit a property before you make the decision to live there.

When living off campus, take extra care for your safety. Don't let strangers know that you live alone if you do not have roommates. For example, on your answering machine message say, "We are not home now" to give the impression that several people live in your apartment. Similarly, only put your last name on your mailbox.

## Landlords

Many students underestimate the relationship with a landlord. This person not only collects your rent—he should also repair problems in your apartment, take care of the entire property, and decide what portion of your security deposit you get at the end of your lease. Sometimes a landlord will be a reference for you when you move on to new housing, such as moving to another city after graduation. Some landlords are very attentive, and others neglect their properties and tenants. Ask your landlord about the security deposit and how he will decide how much you get back, and if possible get that agreement written into the lease. You should also ask the landlord for references and contact the people on that list. Questions you want to ask references include:

- How quickly are repairs made?
- How easy is it to get in touch with the landlord?
- How are the properties cared for?
- How quickly are emergencies addressed?
- How often does the landlord contact tenants?

Some college housing offices maintain a list of landlords. Occasionally, a housing office or student association will provide a rating of local landlords and their properties. The research you do regarding your landlord can keep your living situation simple, allowing you to focus on your studies and social life.

## Utilities

In some cases, utilities are included with your rent. If they're not included, it will be up to you to contact each utility company and arrange for service to your apartment. This can consume your time but needs to be done prior to moving. Keep in mind that you will need to contact some utility companies several weeks in advance of your move-in date. When creating your budget, you also need to allow for utility costs, and be sure to note whether utilities payments are due monthly, quarterly, or by some other schedule. Utilities and other services that you will probably need or want include:

- Electricity
- Water
- Heating fuel
- Waste removal
- Telephone service
- Cable television service
- Internet service

Remember to find out from these companies how quickly faulty service can be repaired, how a service representative can be contacted, and the method in which you will be billed. Many companies now offer online payment options instead of billing by mail. If you do choose an online option, make sure you keep a written log of your payments for your own records and security.

## Getting Around Town

The larger the city you are moving to, the more options you will have as far as shops, restaurants, and other sources of entertainment are concerned. However, a larger town or metropolitan area also requires more time and effort to get acquainted with it. To help you get around, you'll want to take several drives or walks around the area, collect information from your RA or other college staff, and obtain several maps to guide you while you adjust to the new setting.

### Maps

First and foremost, you will need a map of your campus. Usually orientation materials will include a campus map, but if you do not have one, ask your RA where you can obtain one. A map of your campus will help you get to classes, meetings, and college facilities in a timely fashion. A general street map of your college town or city is also a good idea. When trying to find a theater, shopping area, or restaurant you will likely have only an address to guide you. The local chamber of commerce may have a map of area businesses that can help you locate specific places, but a street map will come in handy if you must travel to a professor's house for a club meeting or if you get a local babysitting job. Visitor's bureaus or tourist information centers often have a variety of maps that include local attractions and resources.

**FACT**

You can supplement your map collection with online services. If you are looking for a particular company you can use online phone directories to call for directions. You can also plan trips or get local directions through services such as ✐*www.mapquest.com* and ✐*www.maponus. com.* Just remember that the Internet is an intangible resource and may not be as reliable as a standard map.

It's also a good idea to have an atlas for your car or for taking trips with friends. Travel groups such as AAA can often provide you with a travel map and specific directions. If you're taking a trip with friends in multiple cars, be sure that all the drivers are referring to identical or very similar maps. And remember that maps take up very little space in your room or car, so grab as many as you can. You'll be glad you have them if you ever end up in unfamiliar territory.

## Shopping and Pharmaceutical Needs

It will take almost no time for you to discover that you need to go shopping. You may need to stock your refrigerator, pick up a few toiletries that you forgot, or just get away from campus for a while. Your RA can tell you where students typically shop and how to get to the local shopping areas. She can also tell you where the nearest pharmacy is located. If a cold or flu ever takes you by surprise or if you should need to refill a prescription, you'll want to know how to handle the situation.

While at college, your primary health care resource will be your campus health center. The health center staff can provide basic health care and refer you to specialists in the area. They will also be able to explain how your insurance plan corresponds with their services, as well as with various local pharmacies and doctors. Keep in mind that viruses such as the flu tend to sweep through campuses in waves, so when you head to the health center for some medical attention you will likely find the waiting room full of students who are suffering in a similar manner. Call ahead for an appointment to reduce your waiting time, and bring a book to study while you wait for your turn.

You'll be able to find many basic items at a local grocery store or even at the campus convenience store. Staples like tissues, toothbrushes, and even some over-the-counter medications will probably be available somewhere on campus. But other medications and prescriptions will only be available at a local pharmacy. Before you leave home, go to your preferred pharmacy and find out if they have a branch near your college. If so, then you may not have to transfer your prescription to a new store or have your doctor fill out a new prescription. Whether you switch pharmacies or not, you will want to find one that is close to campus, has a variety of products, and preferably has extended hours.

It's a good idea to tell your RA about any health conditions you have or prescription medications you are taking. He will keep the information confidential, and his knowledge may be useful if you ever have a problem. If your condition or medication is familiar to him, he may also be able to offer suggestions on how to adapt your health constraints to college life.

## Campus Safety

Colleges are generally safe places if you do your part in taking care of yourself and your belongings. One of the simplest things you can do to keep safe is lock your door. Whether you live off campus or in a residence hall, your door should always be locked when you're not home and when you're sleeping. Even a quick trip to the lounge to get a candy bar is enough time for someone to get into your room and take your wallet, your books, or anything else in plain view. On a weekend night, a disoriented student returning from a party could accidentally wander into your room and create a disturbance. Keeping your door locked can help prevent such a situation.

Your college will employ RAs and security officers who routinely patrol buildings to check that doors are not propped open, alarm systems are functioning properly, and dangerous situations, such as broken windows, are addressed promptly. But college staff cannot be everywhere at once. Therefore, it's up to you to secure your belongings and alert staff about unauthorized or suspicious persons on and around your campus.

**QUESTION?**

**Can you take self-defense classes on campus?**
Many campuses offer self-defense courses through the physical education department or security office. If your campus doesn't formally offer such courses, ask your RA to bring in an instructor to teach the residents basic self-defense tactics. You can also check with the local YMCA to see if they have a self-defense class you can take.

Another way to stay safe on campus is to walk in groups of at least two people, especially at night. If you are alone after dark and need to get across campus, call your security office and ask for an escort. Your campus is probably safe, but your personal well-being is too important to take chances with. Also, as you and your friends are walking about campus and the local community be aware of your surroundings. If someone seems to be following you, stop at a store and give the suspicious person a chance to pass. Try to walk in well-lit areas on main travel routes, avoiding alleys and isolated locations.

Some students like to carry personal safety devices, such as pepper spray. Check with your security office to see if such items are permitted on campus. If they are, be sure that you know how to use these items—too often they can be slow to activate or turned against the victim. A whistle is a good safety device, but only if you use it strictly for emergencies. Local residents will quickly learn to ignore false alarms.

## Homesickness and Stress

Before you have been at college very long, you will realize that there really is no place like home. It's not that you will be unhappy with college life; you will just miss family, old friends, and much of the life you used to know. You can feel homesick whether you are having a great time at college or are struggling to adjust. General feelings of stress will also plague you periodically throughout your college career. Stress will result from academic pressures, social situations, and managing your transition to adulthood. Though most stressors will dissipate with the passage of time, the feelings associated with stress can be overwhelming. The good news is that there are a variety of readily available resources for managing stress and homesickness.

Always remember that sadness is normal and manageable. It is when your feelings start affecting your ability to sleep, eat, study, and interact with others that you need to seek help. If you are only experiencing normal feelings of sadness and loneliness, reach out to a new friend for comfort. Chances are she feels similarly and would appreciate a friend as well.

## *Talk It Out*

A prominent resource for coping with homesickness and stress is your roommate and your new group of friends; they will be experiencing many of the same feelings as you. Sometimes a simple conversation as you walk across campus, a discussion over lunch, or a late night gathering in your room is all it takes to put things in perspective. But be warned that group unhappiness can be dangerous. Someone in the group must be able to point to solutions and positive aspects of your current experience. Try watching a favorite comedy or playing a game as a distraction from the present difficulty.

Another resource available to you is your RA. Not only has this upper-class student already been through what you are experiencing, she has been trained to help students in your situation. Experienced RAs have probably been approached about stress and homesickness dozens of times. If there is a general malaise affecting the floor, your RA can organize a program for everyone. If you prefer individual attention, your RA can talk you through what you are feeling and offer constructive suggestions.

**ALERT!**

Constantly calling family or friends will not help if you are homesick. Doing this won't allow you to make the transition to your new life. Call people about once a week and be sure to discuss positive as well as negative experiences that you are having. Though they'll miss you, they'll agree a healthy transition is the main priority.

Your campus will also have counseling resources available to you. In addition to the counseling center, there may be a college chaplain on campus. These professionals are not only highly trained counselors, but they also work with college students every day. Your conversations with them are confidential and are usually covered by college fees. Call ahead to make an appointment with a counselor and don't allow yourself to feel embarrassed about seeking help. The sooner you sort out your feelings, the sooner you can focus on your studies, your social life, and your future.

## Get Involved

When you are stressed out or homesick, it's very important that you stay on campus. If you go home each time you start to struggle you will never learn how to work through the difficulties you are experiencing. Another plus of staying on campus through tough times is that you'll find more opportunities to get involved in college life. Joining a campus organization gives you a chance to meet new people and contribute to a cause. Some organizations and clubs can also provide comforting connections to your old life. For example, if you sang in a choir at home consider joining a college choir or *a cappella* group. If you worked on your high school newspaper or yearbook, join the same group at college. Don't be afraid to try new things as well. You could learn to play rugby or water polo, or join a political organization. Any involvement on campus will take your mind off your troubles and introduce you to new activities and friends.

Physical exercise, whether it is achieved through playing a sport or working out at a gym, can also cause stress to dissipate. Exercise keeps your body strong and energized, which can help you manage the rigors of a college lifestyle. It's also a reason to leave your room and interact with lots of new people. If you're having trouble motivating yourself remember that the hardest part of exercising is getting started. Once you've established a routine, you will see the benefits right away. Force yourself to leave your room and follow a regular exercise schedule. You should also consider group exercise opportunities, such as intramural athletics and jogging partnerships. A healthy body will bring you one step closer to a healthy mind.

## Depression

If your homesickness or stress lasts for more than a couple of weeks, or if you feel generally sad for an extended period of time, you may be depressed. Depression is different from sadness because it lasts longer, runs a bit deeper, and often requires outside help to be resolved. Most people experience depression at several points in their lives and are able to manage the experience successfully, often without medication. If you think you might be depressed, you should make an appointment to speak with a counselor on campus. Your counselor can help identify what is causing your depression, help you develop some healthy coping skills, and refer you to other resources if necessary. Remember that your visit with a counselor is confidential; friends, family, professors, and administrators will not know what happens during your appointment. You are free to be as open and honest as possible.

**QUESTION?**

**What if your roommate or new friends are depressed?**
Trying to cheer up a depressed friend may help initially, but if the depression persists encourage him to seek professional help. You alone cannot be responsible for how a friend is feeling. Be supportive as he works through his depression, but don't let it become the focus of your friendship.

If you choose to tell family and friends that you are depressed you will probably need to guide them through your experience. Are you sharing this with them because you want solutions, want someone to listen, or just think they should know? Would having them come visit campus be helpful? Once you tell family and friends that you are depressed tell them if you are getting outside help and what else you are doing to pull yourself through this time. Most importantly, tell them what you don't want. For example, if you don't want friends on campus to know that you are struggling, ask your family not to send cards, packages, or flowers to help cheer you up.

The most important thing to remember is that depression is manageable and very often temporary. If you are vigilant about taking care of yourself, you can correct the situation without causing a major disruption in your life. Working through one episode of depression will also prepare you to deal with similar problems you or a loved one may have in the future.

## A New Relationship with Your Parents

You will always be your parents' child, but as you become an adult your relationship with them is going to change. While at college, you will still rely heavily on your parents for financial and emotional support. However, you will no longer depend on them for day-to-day help and you will have significantly less contact with them. If you are the first or last child in your family to go to college, this transition may be particularly difficult at first. Your parents will have to adjust to your absence and new independence, and you will need to find support in new places.

At some point during your first semester of college send your parents a card thanking them for their love and support. Tell them how much you appreciate all that they have done for you throughout your life. Not only will this card come as a pleasant surprise, your parents will cherish it for years to come. You may even see it on the refrigerator the next time you go home.

After you have been at college awhile, you will become accustomed to your new independence. Consequently, going home for a break, particularly an extended break, can be a bit of a shock to you and your parents. Do they expect you to follow the rules you had while in high school? Are you hoping to come and go as you please, eat what you want from the refrigerator, and sleep all day? Before heading home for your first break, have an open discussion with your parents about what the expectations are. Some limits may still remain, but you should be able to negotiate a plan that works for everyone.

One thing you will quickly realize is just how smart your parents are. During high school you probably felt that you knew almost everything you needed to know, and your parents were a little out of touch. But by the time you finish your first semester of college, you will be amazed by how many important things your parents know about relationships, time management, budgeting, school work, and even having fun. This is the time for you to start engaging your parents as an adult child, through something more akin to friendship than a subordinate relationship. Share with them some of the things you are experiencing at college, and be open to hearing their thoughts and answering their questions. You may find that you really like your parents, even if you wouldn't choose to go back and live at home again.

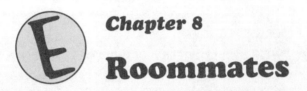

**Chapter 8**

# Roommates

Your roommate may be the person who wakes you up when you sleep through your alarm, who takes messages for you, and who brings you soup when you are sick. She may get you invited to great parties and get you involved in clubs or sports. Your roommate might lend you her favorite clothes, swap jewelry with you, and keep you up laughing for half the night. Or your roommate might simply be the person you share a room with for a few months. In any case, this person will be an important figure in your life.

## *Roommate Selection*

Some colleges will give you a choice between picking your own roommate and being randomly matched with another person. This is a big decision and you should consider it carefully. Picking your own roommate may give you a greater sense of control, but this decision often backfires for students. A randomly selected roommate can become your best friend or your worst enemy, or she may fall somewhere in between.

Schools that allow you to select your own roommate will take one of two approaches. Through one option, you can select a person you know. This may be a friend from high school or your home community. He may also be someone you met during a campus visit. As long as each of you requests the other, your school will probably place you in the same room. It may seem wise to live with someone you know, but keep in mind that living with someone is entirely different than just being his friend. The better you know a person, the more difficult it may be to manage the conflicts that arise.

**QUESTION?**

**What if your random roommate's tastes are radically different from yours?**
Keep in mind that you were likely paired intentionally—the housing staff probably hoped that you could learn from one another. Focus on finding things that you have in common and build on those. Even if you dress differently or enjoy opposing forms of entertainment, perhaps you both appreciate the same foods or have similar study habits.

If you choose to live with a friend, you should first have a long conversation with her about how you're going to manage your room and your friendship. Can you resolve disagreements without dragging mutual friends into the conflict? What if your shared interests begin to diverge and you start to head in different directions? Because you're already friends, how much time do you expect to spend with each other while at college? You need to address these issues as soon as possible so that you can make an informed decision and move on.

Even if you and a friend plan to attend the same college, there are benefits to deciding to live apart. If your friend lives elsewhere on campus you will have another place to visit, you can double the number of people you meet, and it will likely be easier to preserve your valued friendship. After a semester of college, once you know what living with a roommate is all about, if you and your friend still want to try living together, it is probably worth a shot.

The second way that some colleges allow students to pick roommates is through online systems. Through this option you can create a personal profile, view the profiles of other students, and locate individuals with similar interests. Once you've identified a few potential matches, you'll be able to contact them and eventually narrow down your choices to someone you'd like as your roommate. This process comes with many of the drawbacks of online dating—you must trust what people say about themselves and your first meeting is never in person. Online roommate selection can be even more complicated since a date only lasts for a few hours and a roommate is likely to be around for several months.

**ALERT!**

Though a rare occurrence, it's possible that even after you've begun getting to know your roommate over the phone or through e-mail, he will make the decision not to attend your college after all. If this happens, contact your housing office as soon as possible. You'll be matched with a new roommate quickly so you can adapt to this change before move-in day. And do not be discouraged; it was most likely a personal decision that had nothing to do with you.

The most common way that students receive roommates is through an assignment by the college. In this case, you will be asked to fill out a survey, usually only a few questions, detailing your interests and preferences in several categories. The staff at your college will match you with someone based on the similarities found in your surveys. The staff may also take into account your class selection, your major, or your interest in a sport. Some schools work diligently to match roommates with a few similarities and a few distinct differences. For example, you could be matched with someone who shares your taste in music and books but is from a different part of the country.

If you are going to have a randomly assigned roommate, you need to do a few things up front. First, complete your survey as soon as possible and return it to your housing office in advance of the required deadline. Second, complete the survey alone and as honestly as possible. Only you know the truth about your preferences, interests, and pet peeves. Being honest gives your roommate relationship the best chance to succeed. Third, keep in mind that many of the things you mark on the survey will change in the first few months of college. The same is true for your roommate. For example, you may note that you typically go to bed at 10:00 P.M., but at college you might regularly stay up past midnight. Be prepared to manage these changes in yourself and your roommate.

## Initial Expectations

Most housing professionals believe that a student has equal chances of satisfaction with her roommate, regardless of what matching method is used. This suggests that the success of your roommate relationship is mostly up to you. One way to ensure such success is by managing your initial expectations. Be realistic about your new roommate. This person is probably just as excited, nervous, and naive as you regarding college, roommates, and future plans. When you first start living together, most initial conflicts and annoyances will be glossed over. Neither of you will want to make a bad impression or be a bad roommate. Taking this into account, be patient with yourself and your roommate as you get to know each other those first few weeks.

Most students come to college believing that conflict should be avoided. This unrealistic impression can make roommate relations very difficult. Be prepared to disagree with your roommate and plan to work through your differences. Honest, private conversations will solve most of your problems, and your RA will help with the rest.

Most expectations become self-fulfilling prophecies, and many are based on incomplete information. For example, if you immediately decide that you aren't going to like your roommate, you probably won't. And if you learn that your roommate likes classical music, you may picture an antisocial geek with no sense of humor. Don't be too hasty. One piece of information coupled with your desire to figure everything out at once will lead to erroneous expectations. Be patient with yourself and your roommate, and be prepared to change your opinion several times throughout your roommate relationship.

## Making Contact

If you select a roommate, you will already be in touch with that person and will probably begin working out details immediately. If you are matched with a random person, you should get in touch with him soon after receiving his contact information from your school. Most schools will send you your roommate's name, address, and phone number. In recent years many colleges have included e-mail addresses as well, particularly if both roommates have already been assigned college e-mail accounts.

Your initial contact with your new roommate, by whatever means, should be fairly generic. You want to get to know this person and let her get to know you, but neither of you wants to overwhelm the other. Here are some questions to ask during your first conversation:

- Why did you choose this college?
- How many brothers and sisters do you have? Are they older or younger than you?
- How are you spending your summer?
- Do you know what you want to major in yet?
- Are you involved in sports, theater, band, or other activities?
- When can you talk again?

In your next conversation you want to get to know this person a little better and begin to plan for move-in day. You probably want to wait to ask about preferences, such as having guests in the room or how loud to play music, unless these things are deeply important to you. Questions you could ask during the second conversation include:

- What do you like to do for fun?
- How would you like to decorate the college room?
- Which appliances or decorations can you bring on move-in day?
- Do you know anybody else who will be attending the college?
- What classes are you planning to take?

Between phone conversations you should send an occasional e-mail to your new roommate. You don't want to appear too eager, but you do want to continue to get to know this person better. Prior to arriving on campus you should have at least one more phone conversation with your roommate. This final conversation can cover more personal territory and include some of the following questions:

- Are you in a relationship? If so, will your significant other be visiting the room often?
- What kind of social life are you hoping to find at college?
- What is your favorite movie, book, or song and why?
- What will you miss most about your family?
- What are you most looking forward to about college?

If you lay the groundwork for a friendship with your roommate, you will increase your chances for a successful living arrangement. And by discussing important matters before you even arrive at school, you can avoid messy arguments and set the tone for open roommate communication.

**FACT**

Many roommates choose e-mail as their first means of contact. This is less personal than a phone call, but it is a good way to break the ice and start identifying similarities. Your first e-mail or letter should include a basic introduction and suggest a time when you'd be available for a phone conversation.

# Roommate Agreements

During your first few weeks of college, you and your roommate may get along perfectly. But before long academic stresses, conflicting schedules, boyfriends and girlfriends, or a lack of space may begin to complicate things. The best time to start working on conflict is before the conflict actually occurs, and this proactive approach can begin with a roommate agreement.

Your RA may approach everyone on the floor about completing and posting formal roommate agreements. If this is the case, begin with the form your RA provides. If your RA does not provide a form, sit down with your roommate and write down a few issues that are important to each of you. Some of these items may include:

- Sharing CDs, DVDs, and books
- Sharing clothing
- Sharing food
- Items that are off-limits
- Using each other's computers
- Taking phone messages

After you have come to a consensus about these smaller points you need to address more personal issues; these include things like privacy, sleep schedules, and visitor guidelines. These points will be harder to negotiate because they affect each of you more personally. Be honest about your desires and listen carefully to your roommate's views. If you are unable to come to agreement on an issue, ask your RA for guidance.

Your initial roommate agreement will get you through the first round of conflicts, and each of you will likely point out a violation of the agreement. As the semester wears on, you and your roommate will begin to change and something you hadn't covered will inevitably become an issue. For example, if your roommate begins dating someone a few months into the school year, you may feel that this person's visits are infringing upon your privacy. If you didn't address the issue of significant others in your initial agreement, an amendment will likely need to be made at this time.

Every few weeks, you and your roommate should spend a few minutes discussing your roommate relationship and revising your initial agreement. Delete items that are no longer pertinent and add the items that have become relevant. As you get to know each other better you may find more issues that need to be managed before they become conflicts. However, do not use your roommate agreement to address pet peeves. If your roommate's laugh annoys you, there isn't much you can do about it in a roommate agreement. Be realistic in these situations.

Initially, roommates tend to be too general when negotiating agreements. For example, each will agree to "respect" the other without defining that term. In fact, such concepts can have very different meanings, depending on where a person grew up and how she was raised. Be as specific as possible when discussing each item in your agreement.

## Managing Conflicts

No matter how well you get to know your roommate before arriving on campus or how well you design a roommate agreement, some kind of conflict will undoubtedly arise. This may be something trivial that simply annoys you or something much more serious. Whether the conflict occurred because someone put an empty milk carton back in the fridge or one roommate stole the other's stereo, every issue needs to be resolved.

If the conflict is minor sit down with your roommate as soon as possible and discuss the issue—talk about why you are concerned and listen to what she has to say. After you have each had a chance to speak, work together to find a solution. If your conflict is more heated, you might be best served by stepping away for a while and calming down. However, do not complain to other friends about what is happening. Long after the conflict has been resolved, your friends will remember the things you said about your roommate and may even repeat your harsh words. Then you could have another conflict to deal with. Instead, take a walk, call your family to vent (and explain that you are only venting, not asking for solutions), or go work out at the gym. Once you have calmed down, approach your roommate about the situation. Again, explain your views and why the situation upset you so much, and then give your roommate a chance to respond. If she becomes upset, ask if she wants to take a break before discussing the situation further. But don't let things fester for long before you continue your conversation and work on a resolution.

Your college will also provide you with a great resource for working through roommate conflicts: your RA. This student has lived through what you are experiencing and has taken the RA job in order to help others. All RAs receive formal and informal training about roommate conflicts. So, when you are having difficulty with your roommate, knock on your RA's door and ask for some time to talk privately. Be completely open with your RA—she will keep your problem confidential.

**ALERT!**

People deal with conflict in very different ways. Some get angry, shout, and then forget about it. Others keep quiet and address the issue only after significant thought. Find out how your roommate deals with conflict and then explain your own approach. Keep these different styles in mind as you work through your differences.

Your RA can approach your roommate conflict in several ways. If the problem is manageable, your RA will most likely choose to act as a moderator while the two of you talk things out. If the issue is more serious or involves physical or emotional health, your RA may choose to refer you to a counseling service on campus. Your RA's ultimate goal is to have each roommate learn conflict resolution skills so that future problems can be dealt with more peacefully. One important thing to remember is that your RA is a student, just like you. She attends classes, goes to parties, and travels home on breaks. Though she will do everything she can to help you resolve your roommate conflict, she only has so much time and energy to spend on your problems. For this reason, you should always try to resolve a conflict on your own before soliciting your RA's assistance.

## Room Changes

On rare occasions roommates will come to have irreconcilable differences. If this occurs you will need to communicate the problem to your RA, your hall director, and perhaps someone else from your housing office. If everyone agrees that the situation cannot be remedied the only solution is to separate you.

**QUESTION?**

**Which roommate moves when a conflict is irreconcilable?**
If the roommates cannot agree then the housing office will make the decision. The outcome will have nothing to do with money, grades, or personal connections to college staff. Many times the housing office will decide that the only fair thing is to move both roommates.

The decision to separate two roommates comes with complications. First, roommates will likely have to agree on a new living situation. If neither roommate has a replacement living situation in mind, the housing office will have to move one or both students out of the room. This change may discourage some students—they may fear their new roommate situations will be just as bad, or worse, than the first. Additionally, neither roommate will likely want to leave his present floor or residence hall. However, due to a shortage of available space, at least one roommate might have to leave the place he has come to call home.

It is often harder for new students to change rooms in the fall semester. Residence halls are generally filled to capacity at this time, and there may be a waiting list for open rooms. If you're aware of a housing shortage on your campus, you need to be proactive and present your hall director or housing office with a solution. If you and your roommate can find another pair of roommates that wants to split, you can propose a simple swap. In this case, everyone involved must agree about who will be moving into which room. This can be a great solution, but it will require you and your roommate to work together until a consenting pair is found.

## *Lasting Relationships*

Your roommate will definitely be a big part of your college life, but she might also become a bridesmaid in your wedding, a godparent to your child, or a lifelong travel partner. These meaningful relationships don't occur just because you and your roommate listed similar preferences on a survey, or because you had a lot of fun living together for a semester. The roommate relationship, like any other, requires reciprocal attention to survive.

If you and your roommate get along make an effort to keep in touch with each other. If you decide not to live together after your first semester or year, remain friends on campus and try to meet once a week for lunch. If one of you transfers to another school, make a point to visit each other. Meet up at each other's homes or take a quick trip together during break periods. If one of you goes abroad, stay in touch via e-mail and letter writing. If you work to build and maintain the friendship, it should not fade away.

If a friendship with an old roommate gets lost in the shuffle, contact his parents to figure out where he has ended up. Even if you don't know where your roommate has moved or taken up a new job, his parents are bound to have the information. And don't be shy about calling your old friend once you have his number—he has probably been hoping to get in touch with you as well.

After graduation, continue to put the same effort into the friendship. Call and talk to each other at least once a month. If you live far apart, make a point to see each other in person at least once a year. Reminisce together, but also share the things that are current in your life. With enough care and attention, your roommate from freshman year can remain a close friend long after you leave college.

**Chapter 9**

# Clean Room, Clear Mind

You will quickly find that living in a residence hall room is vastly different than living at home. Your bedroom will now be your living room, dining room, kitchen, study, and late-night hang out. Because so much will be going on here, you and your roommate must decide not only how to arrange your furniture, but also how to maximize and maintain the limited space you share.

## *Keeping a Clean Room*

You and your roommate must agree upon how neat or messy to keep your room. If one of you is a slob and the other a neat freak, you are bound to get on each other's nerves from time to time. To manage such differences, it will help if you set some ground rules. For example, agree to dispose of pizza boxes and take-out food containers within twenty-four hours. If one person is not abiding by the rules you both set, the issue should be discussed right away. Remember that it is not only the two of you who will be spending time in your room; you will likely invite friends over to watch movies or play games from time to time.

With all the studying you'll have to do, you won't have time to keep your room immaculate. This is okay, but keep in mind that friends are more likely to hang out in your room if it is relatively clean and there are places for them to sit. You can leave study materials out on your desk and a sweatshirt draped on the back of your chair, but if you have piles of dirty clothing on the floor, people will not feel comfortable in your room. You don't have to empty your trash every day, but perishable food will begin to smell if left in the garbage for too long.

Plastic storage boxes under your bed are a great way to keep things organized and protected, as well as to move items to and from college. A plastic tray or cup will help you keep pens in one place, and a small bottle or bucket will keep loose change and laundry money available for use. Also, hooks on the back of the door are an ideal way to store bathrobes and jackets.

There are a few specific items that you should have in your room to keep it looking and smelling clean. First, it's a very good idea to have a can of air freshener on hand. This can help you mask the odor of Chinese food that may remain after you've eaten it, or you can spray it into your garbage can every time you change the bag. A spray bottle of glass cleaner or all-purpose cleaner will also be helpful. If you spill juice on the floor, this will get rid of any stickiness, and you can also use these products to dust the surfaces of your desk, dresser, and mirror. Remember, though, that certain cleaners should not be used on your computer or other electronic devices. Check with your school's technology helpdesk for information on cleaning and protecting these items.

## College Clothing

You already know that you cannot fit your entire wardrobe in your residence hall room at once. Each visit home should include an exchange of clothes you no longer need for those appropriate to the coming season. The key is to bring as little as possible when you first go to college, without giving yourself too few clothes to choose from.

**QUESTION?**

**What should you wear to class?**
This choice is truly up to you. Some students will wear pajamas to class and others will wear a nice shirt and pants. As a general rule, you should dress comfortably. However, keep in mind that your clothing may send a message to your professor and other students about your personality and attitude.

Starting with the basics, you should plan to have about ten or twelve pairs of underwear in your room at once. Though you will likely wash your clothes at least once a week, it's always a good idea to have some extras on hand. This same rule of thumb applies to socks. There will be times, such as when you exercise, when you will change at least once in the same day. As far as outerwear is concerned, it is a good idea to have a couple of sweaters in your closet at all times, and possibly more during colder months. One or two sweatshirts are sufficient for most college students. A lightweight jacket is a good idea for temperate seasons, and you will need a heavier coat for winter. You really only need one hat and one pair of gloves, but if you have room to store them, an extra set will come in handy if your first set gets lost or wears out.

The informal dress code on most college campuses is casual. Students wear what is comfortable or clothing that fits their individual style. There will be a few occasions when you will need or want to dress up, but how much formal wear you bring is dictated more by your style preference than anything else. You should probably bring several pairs of everyday pants and about three times as many everyday shirts. Remember that you will accumulate T-shirts while at college, so you can bring fewer of those than you might prefer. You should be able to get through about a week and a half before you run out of clean clothes.

Shoes are an individual choice, but keep in mind that they take up a lot of space. You will definitely need at least one pair of each of the following: sneakers for exercise and athletics; flip-flops for the shower; dress shoes; and everyday shoes, such as loafers or walking sneakers. You may want hiking boots, if that is one of your interests, special shoes for biking, cleats for soccer or football, and other additional footwear. If sandals are your style, then you should absolutely bring a pair. Some students choose to have a pair of slippers for wearing around the residence hall, but this is up to you.

It is necessary for you to bring pajamas or some other sort of nightwear. Residence halls are communal environments and you will need something appropriate to wear when you head to the bathroom in the middle of the night, or when you have to go outside for a fire drill at 4:00 A.M. You may choose to use T-shirts and sweatpants for sleeping, but make sure you plan for this when you pack. A bathrobe is a good idea too, particularly if it has pockets where you can keep your room key while you are in the shower.

## Laundry Basics

It turns out that doing laundry is just a little more complicated than throwing clothes in the washer, adding some detergent, and coming back later to put everything in the dryer. Or rather, it is a little more complicated if you want your clothes to look good and last for a while. In order to keep your clothes in good shape you'll need to work out a laundry schedule, learn to sort your clothes according to material and color, and organize a laundry budget.

The first thing you should do is figure out how often you need to do laundry. Don't wait until you're wearing your last pair of clean underwear to drag a heaping basket to your residence hall laundry room. A good rule of thumb is to do laundry once a week. Keep in mind that everyone else in your residence hall will have to do laundry as well, and there will probably only be one machine for every thirty students. Weekend afternoons and Sunday nights are typically peak laundry times in residence halls, so consider choosing another time to avoid the crowds. If you can stick to a consistent laundry schedule, you will be better able to manage your time and will always have something clean to wear.

If you borrow clothing from a friend, it is appropriate to wash the clothing before returning it. Items such as sweaters may not need to be washed unless they have acquired a stain or smell of smoke. If you cause damage that cannot be easily repaired, you should replace the garment.

Next, you need to sort your clothing into groups by color and material. Read the tags on your clothing to see if any items warrant special care; if so, place those items in a separate pile. At the very least, you should separate light and dark colors. Whenever possible, you also want to separate delicates from heavier items. While you are sorting your clothes, be sure to go through all your pockets, remove pins or stickers you placed on your clothing, and tie drawstring ends together. Tying up drawstring ends (on a hooded sweatshirt, for example) will keep the string in place throughout the washing and drying process. Also, be sure that each pile of laundry is the right size. Too few items will waste water in the washing cycle, and too many items can overload the washer and keep the dryer from being effective.

Next, you must choose a detergent. There are a lot of detergents to choose from, and you can select one based on brand, fragrance, price, and so on. While this can get complicated due to the array of detergent, bleach, and pretreating products that exist, a simple general-purpose detergent is sufficient for most college students. You also have a choice between powder and liquid laundry detergents. One advantage of powders is that they take up less space in your residence hall room. However, some people find that powders clump, which can sometimes lead to poor laundry results. Liquid detergents come in large plastic jugs that take up more space, but they won't clump. The best thing to do is try both options and see which one you like better. In any case, thoroughly read the directions for your chosen laundry detergent before using it.

**QUESTION?**

**Should I use a laundry bag or laundry basket?**
Both work well for holding dirty clothes and getting to and from the laundry room. However, a laundry basket takes up valuable space in your car and your room. A laundry bag can be shoved into smaller spaces, even when it is full. If you have the option, choose a bag.

Once you're standing in front of the washing machine, you will have a few more decisions to make. When do you add the detergent and what temperature should the water be? If you're using powder detergent, you generally want to add the detergent after the washing machine has started to fill with water. This will give the detergent some time to dissolve in the water before you add your clothes. Liquid detergent does not require much time to dissolve, so you can choose to add it before or after you put in your clothes. The correct water temperature depends upon what type of clothing you are washing. Many clothing labels will list what temperature the water should be, and college laundry rooms often have temperature guides posted on the walls to assist you. A good rule of thumb is to use cold water for dark colors and new clothes, hot water for whites or particularly dirty clothes, and warm water for everything in between.

Once your load has been washed, you will put it in the dryer. As a rule, you should always empty the lint filter before and after you use the dryer. A clean lint filter allows the dryer to be more efficient, drying your clothes more quickly and completely. A clogged filter is also a safety hazard, particularly when a dryer is being used with high heat settings or very large loads. Every year there are small fires in laundry rooms that could have been prevented if students emptied the lint filters.

**QUESTION?**

**What if the washer or dryer malfunctions?**
Sometimes a machine will take your money but not function properly, or something else may go wrong. If there is no service phone number posted in the laundry room, ask your RA how to report the problem. Meanwhile, you still have to finish your laundry, so pick a different machine and try again.

Remember that most college washers and dryers require money to operate. However, some schools build the cost for laundry into your college fees and set their machines to run without direct payment. In these cases you can usually get your money's worth by doing sixteen to twenty loads of laundry each semester. Other schools use a card system in which the machine debits your charge from a central account. Whatever method your school uses, be sure to find out what is required of you before arriving on campus.

Many colleges and most laundromats still require quarters for each load you wash. If this is your situation then save your quarters every time you get change back from a purchase. You can expect that a load of wash will cost between $0.75 and $1.50, and you'll be charged a similar amount for a cycle in the dryer. Always have extra quarters on hand in case a machine takes your money but doesn't work, or the dryer doesn't dry your entire load in the first cycle. Keep a jar or cup for quarters in a safe place somewhere in your room. Aside from laundry machines, quarters can also be used in payphones and vending machines around campus.

## Laundry Security

One of the big differences between living at home and living away at college pertains to security. Although it may seem that nobody could possibly be interested in taking your clothes, students report theft from college laundry rooms every year. Not only are clothes stolen, but students sometimes find that laundry baskets left in the laundry room get taken as well. To avoid these problems, you can follow a few simple guidelines.

First, don't leave your laundry unattended. Nobody will take your clothes if you're there watching the machines. Read a book, do some studying, or write a few letters to family and friends while your clothes are in the washer or dryer. You and a friend might even choose to do laundry at the same time and keep each other company.

Instead of washing four loads of laundry at once, consider doing two loads one day and the other two a few days later. In doing this, you won't have to drag a ton of heavy laundry down to your laundry room, and you won't risk losing as much clothing to theft or other problems.

Though it is the best way to prevent theft, most college students do not stay in the laundry room throughout the entire washing and drying process. If you will not be in the room where your clothes are being laundered, you should at least remain in the building. That way, whether you go back to your room or wait in the residence hall lounge, you can periodically check on your clothes. You will also have a feel for who else is in the building, so if something comes up missing you will have a better chance of narrowing down possible suspects.

Likewise, it's important to retrieve your clothes as soon as they are done. Leaving a washer full of wet clothes for several hours will only irritate others who are waiting to use the machine. Leaving items in the dryer similarly upsets people waiting to do their laundry and may result in your clothes being moved on top of the machine, to a folding table, or thrown on the floor. Also, clothing left in the dryer long after the cycle has finished is likely to require ironing before it looks presentable. Wrinkles won't be a problem if you hang your clothing as soon as it is dry.

Another way to keep your clothes secure is to write your name or initials on an inconspicuous part of your garments. If you do this, be sure to use a permanent marker that won't bleed through. If you find that some of your clothes are missing from the laundry room, check with other people who were doing laundry at the same time. Sometimes another person can innocently walk off with your clothes. Having your initials written somewhere on your clothing can help you prove that a garment is actually yours. If you can't find a missing item, you should report the incident to your RA and campus security office immediately.

Be careful about accusing someone of stealing your clothing. Due to the size of your campus or the fact that many college students dress similarly, it is likely that someone else will have the exact same piece of clothing that you lost. Unless you can prove that the specific item is yours, you are unlikely to recover any clothing and you might offend any students you wrongly accuse. Also, be particularly thorough when searching for the lost item before you make any accusations. Your roommate or one of your friends may have borrowed the item without asking you first, or perhaps the "stolen" item simply fell beneath your bed when you were sorting your clothing. Don't rush to place blame until you're sure the loss wasn't your own mistake.

## Stains and Other Crises

Whether you're a sloppy eater or just a victim of circumstance, you are likely to find a stain on your clothing, a button missing from your shirt, or a rip in your pants at some point in your college career. While living at home you likely had a family member who could effortlessly resolve these little crises. But now that you are away at college you will have to learn to deal with these problems on your own.

**QUESTION?**

**What do you do with a permanently stained article of clothing?**
If you're unable to remove a stain, don't immediately get rid of the item. You can still use it for exercise, a painting class, or for just hanging out in your room. If you don't want to keep the garment, donate it to an art program or maintenance department that can reuse it.

When you find a stain on your clothing, first try removing the stain with a small amount of laundry detergent or dish soap. Use cold water and be gentle as you work with the stained area. Many times small stains can be resolved this way and you can toss the clothing in with your next load of laundry. If the stain is more persistent or set-in, you need to pretreat the stained area when you are about to do a load of laundry. You can use a small amount of liquid detergent or a pretreating product to do this. Follow the directions on your stain remover and read cautions carefully in case the remover will not work well with a particular kind of stain or fabric. You may need to soak your stained clothing before washing it in order to loosen the soil and give the stain remover or detergent a chance to activate. This can be done using a small bucket of warm water or a presoak feature, if available, on your washing machine.

A local dry cleaner may be the best answer for clothing crises. If you haven't washed the item, the dry cleaner may be able to remove a stain. Point out the stain and tell the staff what it is (food, paint, etc.). Using this method will give you the benefit of clean, pressed clothing, but remember that you'll have to pay for the service.

Before you place your clothing in the dryer, check to see if the stain came out in the wash. If not, do not put the item in the dryer; doing this will only cause the stain to set and likely become permanent. Instead, go back and read the directions on your stain remover regarding persistent stains, or call home and ask your family for advice. It may be that another cycle of soaking and washing will clear up the stain, or else you may be stuck with a stained piece of clothing.

At some point during your college career, it is likely that you will loose a button from a shirt. You can purchase a small sewing kit, complete with several colors of thread and a few needles, at most drug stores, and perhaps even in your college bookstore. If you manage to save the button or find it in the washing machine at the end of a cycle, you can simply sew the button back onto your shirt. If the button is lost, you can often find a replacement at a craft store, and some shirts have spare buttons sewn on the underside of the bottom hem.

For many new students, sewing a button on a shirt is a completely foreign activity. Though it is not nearly as difficult as some of the classes you are taking you may not be able to do it well enough to make your shirt wearable again. If this is the case, inquire with your friends to see if one of them can teach you how to reattach the button. You can also ask an RA for assistance, or visit a local sewing shop in town.

Rips and tears are often harder to deal with and may require waiting until your next trip home to repair. You can easily get an iron-on patch and apply it yourself, but that will only work for some types of clothing. You may also find a tailor at a local dry cleaner who can repair rips and tears easily and for minimal charge. Do not necessarily abandon clothing that has been damaged in this way; just be patient while you figure out the best solution.

## *Ironing*

When packing or shopping for college clothing, remember that most of your time will be spent studying, socializing, and sleeping. You won't want to spend a lot of extra time ironing clothes. To help you avoid this chore, select fabrics that resist wrinkles and plan to hang your garments as soon as they finish in the dryer.

**ALERT!**

Be careful about where you iron your clothes. Residence halls are equipped with heat or smoke detectors that can be easily set off by a hot iron, especially if you use a steam setting. Never iron underneath these devices, and always remember to turn off and unplug your iron as soon as you finish.

Though you will want to avoid ironing whenever possible, certain garments will require ironing or you will want to iron your clothes for the occasional special event. However, not every college has ironing boards in the laundry rooms, and few schools provide irons for students. If many of your clothes require ironing, it's worth it to bring your own equipment. But if you only have a few of these items, you might decide to borrow an iron whenever you need it.

Some students use a steam tool to smooth out wrinkles instead of an iron. These products work fairly well and don't require an ironing board, so this may be a viable alternative for you. The other thing you can do is take your clothing to a dry cleaner to be pressed. This service will cost you extra money, but it will deliver professional results. Still, keeping in mind your time constraints and tight budget, the best option is probably just to borrow an iron or steam tool whenever you need one.

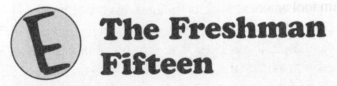

## Chapter 10

# The Freshman Fifteen

On most campuses, "the freshman fifteen" is a term you hear often. This refers to the fifteen pounds that most students allegedly gain during their first year of college. The truth behind this term is debatable, but your eating habits certainly will change dramatically during your first year at college. Most cafeterias offer unlimited servings, so you can choose to eat three helpings of fries with your two cheeseburgers and bowl of ice cream. However, this kind of diet can quickly become a health problem if not monitored and kept in check.

## A Healthy Diet

Healthy eating involves quantity, variety, and frequency of your meals. While your cafeteria may offer a variety of appealing foods for every meal you will need to exercise some self-control. It's important that you only take the amount of food that will fulfill your appetite without making you sick. If you continually overeat, your capacity for food (and your body weight) will likely increase. Each time you make a trip to the serving line or buffet, take only one serving of food. If you are still hungry, you can always return for a second helping. Upon leaving the cafeteria you should no longer be hungry, but you shouldn't be loosening your belt, either.

In addition to eating a reasonable amount of food, you also need to vary the foods that you eat. Fruits and vegetables are important to your body's ability to function and are readily available in the cafeteria. Supplement one serving of an entrée with at least one serving of vegetables, and occasionally consider fruit as a dessert. Don't neglect the other basic food groups, either. Grains and dairy are also important in a balanced diet. Take time to read the nutrition information posted in your cafeteria and try to select meals that hit all of the recommended nutrition points listed.

**QUESTION?**

**Are you unhappy with the selection or service in your college cafeteria?**
Your student government probably has a grievance committee that presents student concerns to the administration. There may also be a food service committee that you can offer suggestions to or join. If you want to see a change, it's up to you to make your voice heard.

There will be a variety of meals available at your college and you should sample as many as possible. Try not to eat fried food for every meal, and don't shy away from sampling dishes you have never heard of, particularly if you are in a new part of the country or on a very diverse campus. This is a chance to explore new foods and cultures. You should also try to plan your meals for the whole day to be sure you're getting the proper nutrition. If you have plans to study and order pizza with friends in the evening, have a large salad for lunch. If you know that you'll be exercising later in the day, be sure to include some protein in your earlier meals. And if you think you are getting a cold, have an extra glass of orange juice with breakfast.

Look for a kitchenette in your residence hall and consider cooking an occasional meal there. You may be able to prepare a family favorite, such as a casserole or meatloaf, which will be nutritious as well as comforting. You may also impress your new friends with your cooking prowess, even if the recipe is actually very simple.

A simple goal is to try to have three well-balanced meals a day, regardless of what you eat between meals. College life is filled with opportunities for snacking, so you need to make a point to eat healthy foods during meals. Even if you keep an active lifestyle, you'll still have to maintain a healthy diet. If you are not particularly active, you will need to pay special attention to your snack intake and dedicate yourself to eating well-balanced meals.

Your college diet is likely to be inconsistent, even when you are vigilant about it. This being the case, you might consider one of the many multivitamins that are available over the counter. It's important to make sure your body is getting the nutrients it needs on a daily basis, and multivitamins offer a one-stop solution for people who aren't necessarily health-conscious. Consult your family physician, pharmacist, coach, or college health center staff for advice on a good multivitamin or other dietary supplement. But remember: Only treat your vitamin as a supplement and not a substitute for healthy eating. If you are taking prescription medication, check with your physician to make sure that the multivitamin you choose won't create any unwanted side effects.

While at college, you may decide to try to lose some weight. The best weight-loss plans are managed through a responsible diet and healthy exercise. Fad diets are typically overrated and can even be dangerous. Any diet that promises fast results with minimal effort should be viewed skeptically. If you don't know how to begin a healthy weight-loss program, talk to your campus health center staff or your physician, or ask your RA to sponsor a program for your floor. Remember, too, that your body is still changing. As you grow into a mature adult, you are inevitably going to look and feel different than you did in high school. You should only choose to go on a diet or join a specific weight-loss program if you have your health in mind. Don't do something drastic or dangerous just to gain the approval of your peers.

## Frugal Eating

After you have been at college for about a month, you will start to see the same things appear in the cafeteria. While the food will taste fine, you will tire of having the same meals every couple of weeks. This is when you and your friends will start eating out more, and consequently, you'll begin spending more money. Each time you eat outside of your meal plan your budget will take a hit, so you need to be careful about what food you purchase and how often. This does not mean you should start eating other people's food or starving yourself to save money. However, you'll need a plan to balance your diet and get your money's worth.

You should tip the person who delivers your food. This person may be a college student, like yourself, or a parent working hard to support a family. Either way, you should always include a few extra dollars when paying for your food. Tipping makes delivered food more expensive, so if you're trying to save money consider picking up the food yourself.

If you are buying snacks for your room, consider store brand items instead of name brands. You probably won't notice a difference in taste but you will appreciate the difference in price. Also, compare the price of a single serving with that of family size items. You may not eat all of those crackers now, but if you buy the smaller box four times you could end up wasting your money. Another money-saving strategy is to check the sales and coupons for your supermarket. Clipping coupons is not very exciting, but think of the $0.50 or $0.75 you save as money in your pocket. Some stores offer a frequent shopper card that gives you the discounts without clipping coupons. However, you should still review the supermarket circulars for special offers.

Another key to frugal eating is saving leftovers. If you get a pizza but end up throwing half of it away, you lose half of your money. If you buy a bag of chips and they go stale, you will not have gotten your money's worth. Buy only what you will eat before the food spoils. Also, invest in some resealable containers. These will keep your food fresh, keep strong odors contained, and prevent the appearance of bugs. Likewise, you can purchase a couple of bag clips to seal off opened bags of chips, pretzels, and other snacks so they don't go stale. Taking these few simple measures will help you get the most bang for your buck.

Occasional sharing is okay, but remember that you need to feed yourself before you feed your friends. If you are constantly buying food that everyone else eats, you'll quickly run out of money. If you enjoy hosting football parties but find the cost of snacks overwhelming, take some of the burden off yourself by asking some of your guests to chip in or bring a snack to share.

When ordering food for delivery, find out which restaurants are the cheapest in the area. Some places may charge a delivery fee, so take that into account when ordering. You can also look for restaurants that offer specials or discounts for college students. Another way to save is by splitting delivery orders with friends. You don't need to eat an entire pizza by yourself, and sharing the cost with friends will save you money. This can also be a great opportunity to socialize with other students on your floor. And keep track of which restaurants offer weekly or nightly specials. For example, if Thursday is "wing night" you might be able to get a standard order of chicken wings for significantly less money.

# Eating Disorders

Eating disorders affect between 1 and 3 percent of the population, and various problems with eating, exercise, and weight affect many more. These illnesses are especially prevalent on college campuses, where physical appearance and popularity are common topics of conversation. Eating disorders can have serious psychological and physical consequences; therefore, college students must be able to recognize signs of an eating problem in themselves and their friends, as well as know where to get help. Fortunately, college campuses provide a variety of resources to help students with eating disorders and others who are concerned about them.

You have probably heard of the two primary types of eating disorders: anorexia nervosa and bulimia nervosa. People suffering from anorexia dramatically restrict their food intake, often consuming only a few hundred calories per day. Their weight may become dangerously low, but they tend to be dissatisfied with their bodies and view themselves as overweight. Bulimics generally eat a large amount of food in a short period of time, while experiencing a sense of a lack of control over their eating. They also engage in purging, which is recurrent behavior intended to prevent weight gain. Some examples of purging are self-induced vomiting, excessive exercise, and misuse of laxatives. A third type of eating problem that has been increasingly noted on college campuses is binge eating disorder. People with this condition engage in repeated binges as in bulimia, but they rarely or never purge. They are usually of normal weight or overweight.

It's easy for students who live close together on a campus to notice one another's eating habits, but it's sometimes difficult to know when unusual eating behavior becomes a cause for concern. Some physical signs that a student may have an eating problem are:

- Visible and/or rapid weight loss or gain
- Frequent complaints of fatigue or feeling cold when others do not
- Scars on hands
- Loss of enamel on teeth (from frequent vomiting)
- Appearance of illness, such as pale complexion, circles under eyes, thinning or dull hair

Some behavioral signs that a student may have an eating problem are:

- Eating very little or not at all
- Frequently eating much more than would be expected at one sitting
- Disappearing after meals or being observed vomiting after meals
- Overusing laxatives, diuretics, or diet pills
- Exercising excessively
- Isolating oneself and curtailing social activities
- Seeming depressed or anxious
- Making negative and distorted comments about own body or weight

A person may or may not recognize an eating disorder in himself; often it is friends or family members who first realize that something is wrong. If you are concerned that a friend may have an eating problem, it is important to discuss it with the person. Present your concerns in a direct and specific manner, but avoid making a diagnosis. For example, you could say, "I've noticed that you rarely eat meals with us anymore, you seem tired and sad, and you look like you are losing weight. I'm worried about you." Suggest that the student consider talking to a professional at the campus counseling or health center. Consider offering to accompany the person to her first appointment.

**FACT**

Eating disorders do not only affect women; men of all ages also suffer from these illnesses. If a male friend is exhibiting signs of an eating disorder, don't ignore the problem just because he is a guy. Address the situation with your friend, contact his family, or obtain advice from a local expert on how to deal with the issue.

When trying to help a friend with an eating problem, you must keep several things in mind. Individuals with eating disorders often deny the seriousness of their problem and may respond with either anger or indifference when you express concern. However, this does not mean you should not pursue the issue. If a friend does not decide to seek help and you remain worried about her, it's a good idea to reiterate your concerns again later. If you are unsure of how to approach a friend you are worried about, or a friend has responded negatively to your approach, head to your health or counseling center for expert advice on how to cope with the situation.

People may live with eating disorders for many years, but in the process they can seriously damage their bodies and endanger their long-term health. A student suffering from a long-term eating disorder may have friends and family at home who are concerned about her, but they may not be able to monitor the situation closely if she is far away at college. Therefore, it is important that you address problems you notice in friends, and contact their families if the situation worsens. Do not, however, take full responsibility for the individual. This will drain you emotionally, and can interfere with your own life and academic plans. Approach your RA, health center staff, or another authority to help you deal with the situation.

## Smart Snacks

While studying for exams, writing papers, or just hanging out with friends, you'll often want a snack. Unfortunately, most of the food available to you outside of the cafeteria qualifies as junk food. Vending machines are filled with carbonated beverages and candy bars that are high in sugar, as well as potato chips that are high in sodium and fat. Delivery food usually consists of pizza, fried foods, and sandwiches that tend to be lacking in nutritional value. So, where can a college student find smart snacks?

Keep a stash of granola bars or another high-protein snack in your room. When you feel a little hungry, grab one of these instead of heading for the vending machine or ordering delivery food. Often a small snack is all you need to quell your hunger and help you regain focus on the task at hand.

First, take a trip to your local supermarket and spend some time in the produce section. Look for fruits and vegetables you can keep in your room. Apples and oranges are quick, delicious snacks that will keep well in your refrigerator. You can also find baby carrots or celery sticks that are ready to eat out of the bag. You might also try dates, apricots, and dried fruits. Sometimes you might find a low-fat or fat-free dip for vegetables that will make them more appealing. Unsalted or lightly salted nuts make a healthy snack, especially when mixed with dried fruit in a trail mix. And you should also consider canned fruits; they will last longer than fresh fruits aand come in many varieties. Of course, you must have or be able to borrow a can opener if you buy canned items.

Your food service office and health center staff should be able to provide you with healthy snacking ideas, and your college gym or athletics department may have a nutritionist on staff to answer your questions. In general, you want to eat light, high-protein snacks, and steer clear of foods with lots of sugar, caffeine, or saturated fats. And choose a glass of water or juice over soda, whenever possible.

## Resisting Temptation

Whether you are sitting in your room, hanging out in the lounge, or having fun at a party you will find that there will always be food nearby. Even receptions and special events on campus often include food. Though free food excites most college students, you will have to learn to resist the temptation to eat whatever is put in front of you. Eating too much junk food will cause you to gain weight and suffer from any of a number of digestive problems, including cramps, diarrhea, and constipation. While these greasy, gummy, crumby foods may be tempting, you'll have to exert some self-control to keep your body healthy.

Self-control is the key concept when it comes to constant munching. If you are not hungry, avoid continually popping snacks in your mouth. If you find that snacking is an unconscious reaction to the presence of food, then remove the food from your sight. Sit far away from the snack bowl, don't keep snacks in your room, and remind yourself that you really aren't hungry. You might even consider chewing gum—you are unlikely to eat snacks if you already have something in your mouth. Some students find that brushing their teeth dulls their desire to eat between meals, and it can only help with dental hygiene. And if you and a friend both suffer from snack cravings, decide to help one another with the problem. If you see your friend reaching for a chocolate bar, remind her that an apple might make a better snack.

When deciding whether to snack or not, keep in mind what you ate that day. If you had healthy meals earlier in the day, then a little nighttime snacking may be okay. But if you ate a cheeseburger for lunch and fried chicken for dinner, an evening snack of potato chips is a bad idea. Use common sense and pay attention to the signals your body gives.

## Healthy Exercise

You have heard that exercise is an important part of a healthy lifestyle. More accurately, healthy exercise is an important part of a healthy lifestyle. Infrequent, intense exercise is unhealthy and can be dangerous to your body and mind. The best way to take care of your body is to engage in moderate exercise regularly. Find out when your campus fitness center is open and visit it two to four times per week. Also, make a point to learn when the center's peak hours are. Some people prefer to go when the gym is empty so they have a greater selection of machines and free weights at their disposal. Others enjoy the sense of community and motivation that comes with working out among a crowd. Whether you prefer to work out in an empty gym or a bustling one, you can plan your schedule around the peak hours.

Your exercise regimen must also take into account your body's current condition. You won't be able to lift 180 pounds safely the first time you work with free weights. And you won't be able to run ten miles on a treadmill if you've never used one before. You need to train your body and work up to a healthy limit. If you need help learning how to use the machines or weights in the gym, ask one of the staff for advice. Many gyms also offer aerobics or martial arts classes to students. Consider these options as alternatives to a solitary workout in the gym.

A regular exercise regimen is an integral part of a healthy college lifestyle. You might consider taking a physical education class to introduce you to college physical fitness and your campus fitness center. Your fitness center may offer one-time classes or orientation to the fitness center. And you can always approach your RA about setting up a program designed to help you and your peers develop personal fitness plans. Once you start exercising, stick to a predictable schedule. Your body will become accustomed to the regular work and will develop and grow stronger over time.

## QUESTION?

**What if you don't like working out in a gym atmosphere?**
College is the ideal time to try new kinds of exercise. Alternative sports, like racquetball or squash, are often available. You might also want to ask a friend to be your jogging partner. Consider taking advantage of local natural resources, such as hiking and biking trails. Or you can join an organized sports team or athletic club, like crew, field hockey, swimming, or soccer.

Your college days will be busy and filled with possibility. But no matter what else you choose to do, you must find the time to exercise, and also find ways to make that exercise enjoyable. It is up to you to motivate yourself and maintain a healthy lifestyle. In doing this, you should see improvements in your physical appearance, your energy level, and even your grades.

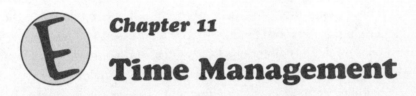

**Chapter 11**

# Time Management

In the past your mother or father may have helped you with your homework, insisted that you practice your musical instrument, or made sure you went to bed at a decent hour. However, while you're away at college, you alone will be responsible for managing your time. This is not impossible to do, but it's not easy either. You will likely have to try a number of time management tactics before you discover a routine that works for you.

## *Start with the Big Stuff*

The best way to begin managing your time is to first consider large or inflexible commitments. One such commitment is your classes. Academic classes are scheduled consistently throughout the semester and your attendance is required to succeed. Other important items on your schedule may include club meetings, team practices, or a job commitment. While these parts of your schedule may be more flexible than your classes, you have a responsibility to your other club members, teammates, and your employer.

Meals are another important item in your schedule. While you have some flexibility concerning when you eat, you are constrained by two things. First, your body needs food on a regular basis. Failure to eat will not only deprive you of vital nutrition and energy, but your hunger will become a distraction as you try to focus on other items. Second, your college cafeteria may have limited hours. If you don't get to the cafeteria before it closes, you'll likely miss out on a satisfying meal. Therefore, you should work meals into your schedule at consistent times. If a spontaneous study group meeting interferes with your regularly scheduled dinnertime, try to eat a larger lunch or bring a snack to the meeting to tide you over.

Try thinking of your time commitments as different types of matter. Sleep and class time are like solids and can't be altered easily. Meals, study time, and exercise are like liquid—moveable, but very important. Social time and TV-watching are like gas—easily moved around your other commitments.

Many college students have jobs to help them pay for incidental needs, tuition, or books. Whether your job is on or off campus your employer is going to give you a set schedule. If you fail to abide by this schedule, you may lose your job. A job is a very important commitment and it should be treated as seriously as your classes. However, if a job becomes so stressful or time-consuming that it takes away from your study or class time, you may need to search for a less demanding position.

Another big and inflexible item in some students' schedules is athletics. If you are a member of an intercollegiate team, you will have set practices, weight room sessions, and games or competitions. A commitment to a sport is a serious one, particularly if you are receiving scholarship money for it. But if you are simply engaging in a sport to get in shape or use up extra time, be sure that the commitment does not interfere with your academic performance.

The big schedule item most often neglected by college students is sleep. Now that you dictate your own bedtime, it is tempting to stay up half the night talking with friends, watching movies, or ordering takeout. The truth is that your body needs a minimum amount of sleep each night, and this amount must be kept relatively consistent. This can be particularly difficult if you have an 8:00 A.M. class on Mondays, Wednesdays, and Fridays, but can sleep in on Tuesdays and Thursdays. If this is the case you need to find a medium and do your best to go to bed at similar times every night. Your body will function better if you have a regular routine. It is also important to allow yourself six to eight hours of sleep each night. Consider sleep to be a non-negotiable item in your time management system.

**ALERT!**

No matter how well you take care of yourself, you are bound to get sick at some point during your first year of college. Whether it is a common cold or a full-blown flu, you need to know how to deal with it. Take special care to drink lots of fluids and get plenty of rest while you are sick, and visit your college health center if symptoms become unmanageable.

Don't plan to make up for lost nighttime sleep with daytime naps; the two are not equivalent and sufficient naps are hard to achieve in noisy residence halls. If you are tired during the day consider giving yourself an extra hour of sleep each night or exercising more often to boost your energy. Additionally, avoid pulling all-nighters at all costs. Many students think that all-nighters are a given in college life, but this is not necessarily true. Staying up all night studying for a test or completing a project will only fail you the next day when you cannot keep your eyes open.

## *Wants Versus Needs*

Once you have placed the big items in your schedule, it's time to figure out when you are going to do everything else. It will quickly become apparent that there is not enough time to do everything, and the conflict between "need" and "want" will create tension in your schedule. The key to managing this tension and effectively managing your time is to create a balanced schedule. If you do this successfully, you will be able to tend to all of the "needed" items and most of the "wanted" items, creating a happy lifestyle.

### *Scheduling Your Needs*

There are several important parts of your college life that should always take precedence over leisure activities in your schedule. These needs include: your education, your health, and possibly, your job. These items deserve extra time in your schedule and extra attention in your life. If you don't do well in your classes, take care of your health (both mental and physical), and maintain a job (if this income pays your tuition), then your college career could end as quickly as it began.

A tip for keeping a balanced schedule is to manage your time according to your body's strengths. If you do your best thinking during daylight hours, plan to study then. If you are more of a night owl, you may choose to study in the evening. You should also plan to exercise at a time when you generally have low energy in order to recharge your body.

Above and beyond including class time in your schedule, you will also have to study outside of class. Since your main goal at college is to get an education, you should schedule study time accordingly. If you anticipate an hour and a half of study for every hour of class, and your class meets for three hours each week, then you will need to delegate four and a half hours to study for that class each week. Most colleges recommend at least three hours of study for each hour of class so that students can do the necessary reading, review lecture notes, and prepare for class discussions or presentations. But generally, students find they need to study more for some classes than others, and they adjust their schedules accordingly.

Study time should also be broken up into sections. For example, you don't want to study for the same class for three straight hours. You will have trouble staying focused for that long and will not retain as much knowledge. Try to keep study blocks to about an hour for each class. You can break up study blocks with other activities or take a short break and begin a study block for another class. Look carefully at your schedule and see if there is hidden time that you can use to study as well. For example, if you have class at 10:00 A.M., consider studying for that class each day at 9:00 A.M. right after eating breakfast. Or if the class ends at 11:00 A.M. and you have nothing scheduled until lunch, plan to go to the library and study for that class from 11:00 A.M. to noon. Studying for a class immediately before or after it meets helps you retain the material being covered, and studying during the day-time will allow you more time to relax in the evening.

It is important to take your health as seriously as you take your classes while in college. If you don't get enough sleep, don't maintain a healthy diet, or don't exercise regularly, your studies will inevitably suffer. Remember to pay attention to your body and heed the signs it gives. If you get headaches every time you read for more than an hour, you should consider one hour of reading your maximum before taking a break or moving on to something else. If you find that you are falling asleep in class, you need to try to go to bed earlier. And if your stomach gets upset every time you eat a certain snack food, you should eliminate that food from your diet.

**ALERT!**

Just as important as your physical health is your mental health. If you begin to suffer from extreme stress or anxiety over your classes or grades, you need to reevaluate your situation and seek the advice of an RA, counselor, or friend. Though your reason for being in college is to excel academically, nothing is more important than your health.

Even though your education and your health should be your main priorities, for some students, a job is necessary to pay for college tuition, books, or other needs. If this is your situation, you need to treat your job just as seriously as you do your classes. Abide by your employer's schedule, follow the rules of the institution where you work, and be respectful of your employer and colleagues. If you need a job to afford school but find that your current position is too stressful or time-consuming, look for a replacement position where you can work fewer hours.

## Scheduling Your Wants

Once you have allowed enough time for your needs, be sure to allocate some time to your wants. These activities include extracurricular interests, like sports and clubs, entertainment, such as movies, concerts, and plays, and general relaxation and social time. Though you probably will not have time to participate in every club or sport that interests you, and you won't have enough time (or money) for a weekly trip to the movies, you should be able to find a balance between your needs and wants.

Being a part of a college athletic team is a big responsibility. Aside from presenting a physical challenge, most sports teams require participants to attend practices, meetings, and competitions. If you are interested in playing a sport, but don't want the pressure that comes with playing on a recognized college team, you might want to consider playing intramural sports. Intramural sports are available to all students, regardless of athletic ability, and they generally require far less time and energy. Likewise, if you don't feel you have the time for a position in student government or don't want to be president of a club or organization, consider simply becoming a member of that group. Club members are generally expected to attend weekly or monthly meetings, but they usually aren't required to take on authoritative positions, pay money, or dedicate outside time to the cause. Of course, if you have the time and motivation to become more involved in a club or sport, keep the level of commitment in mind when scheduling other responsibilities.

Other wants you should consider when creating your schedule are leisure activities, such as movies, concerts, and plays. These activities will not appear consistently in your schedule, but you will want to have the option to take advantage of them when they are available. Sometimes these events will be held on campus, and therefore, you won't have to go far or pay an exorbitant amount to attend. Other events, particularly concerts, may be held in another city and will require you to travel. If this is the case, buy your ticket ahead of time, mark the event in your schedule, and plan any other activities around that event.

No matter how many commitments you have, you will need to leave some time unscheduled each day. You can use that time for a meal with friends, a favorite hobby, or even just a nap. If you schedule every minute of every day you will quickly become stressed out. Leaving a few empty spaces in your schedule gives you the freedom to adjust things each day, be spontaneous, or just relax. "Doing nothing" is sometimes the only way to gain the composure you need to get through the day.

Make a list of the fun things you want to do each month, from seeing movies to attending campus events. Then plug those items into your schedule so that you don't forget them or schedule over them. You won't have time to attend every event or see every movie, but you should be able to fit in your first choices.

It is also important to plan your weekends, even if you plan them loosely. Saturday morning is a great time to study, though you should still allow yourself time to sleep in. Saturday afternoons are a good time to do reading for your classes, especially when the weather is nice and you can sit outside somewhere on campus. Sunday evenings are a traditional study time as well. Plan to have Friday and Saturday evenings free to socialize with your friends, and stick to that plan. Weekends are also a great time to take small trips home or to visit friends at other colleges. If you do decide to take a weekend trip, be sure to include travel time in your schedule, and remember that traffic may be heavier than usual on Friday afternoons and Sunday evenings.

Once you have a set schedule, post it somewhere that is highly visible. You may put it over your desk, on a mirror in your room, or on the back of your room door. You want to be able to look at your schedule regularly. It is also important to revisit your schedule every couple of weeks and make adjustments. If your first schedule includes too much study time and not enough time for meals, make the necessary changes when you plan the following week.

## Trading Time Blocks

Your time management schedule will be a guide, but it will rarely work flaw-lessly. While at college you will never know when a good opportunity is going to arise. For example, you may be sticking to your scheduled Tuesday evening hour of biology study when a friend from down the hall invites you to join her for a movie premier. How can you possibly refuse? But if you go to the movie and then return to your regular schedule you will have lost that study block. Where can you make up for the lost time?

Sometimes the key to keeping to your schedule is saying no to friends who want to do other things. Be determined to make your schedule work, and say no to interruptions and distractions. If friends push you, tell them that you will join them when you have finished. Self-discipline is the single most important factor in successful time management.

The trick you need to learn is how to trade time blocks. If you give up your hour of biology study to go out with your friends you need to add an hour of study at a later point in the day or week. Before you head to the movie determine when you will make up the study time. One strategy is to trade similar time blocks. That is, if you forego an hour of study to be social, replace an hour of social activity you had planned for later in the week with an hour of study. If you repeatedly skip study time to be social, you will eventually fall behind in your classes.

The challenge is figuring out when to trade a time block and when to decline an opportunity. You should not repeatedly decline social opportuni-ties. If you do your friends will soon stop asking you to participate in sponta-neous trips or events. Similarly, you can't ignore your study schedule every time an opportunity arises. You must identify the type of opportunity and weigh it against your overall schedule. If your friends ask you to join them at a restaurant but you have already eaten dinner, you should probably decline the offer. But if a group is heading out to see a comedian who is only on campus for one night, you probably want to take advantage of this chance. Trade the study block with a later scheduled social activity.

You also need to keep in mind what is going on in your classes. If you have a test coming up you probably want to decline an opportunity that interrupts preparing for that test. If you have to be at work first thing in the morning, you don't want to stay out late with friends and lose valuable sleep. However, if you know you will simply be watching a film in class the next day, or you are already familiar with the material to be covered, you can probably participate in a social activity the night before. Also, before you head out on weekend trips, be sure to outline any work that needs to be finished by the following Monday. Bring any study materials you need with you on your trip, and find the time to get things done so you aren't rushing to complete an assignment on Sunday night.

**ALERT!**

College professors are generally unsympathetic to excuses such as your alarm didn't go off due to a power failure or your disk was mangled in the computer. If you decide to trade time blocks, be sure you have still allowed yourself enough time to complete an assignment before the deadline. False excuses will only make your professor suspicious.

## Combining Tasks

You will have many opportunities to combine tasks while at college, but you have to be selective about which tasks you combine. Writing a term paper while eating dinner will leave a mess on your keyboard or food all over your notes. However, catching up on your reading while you wait for your laundry to dry may be a very efficient use of your time. Multitasking is a common time management strategy among college students. The challenge is to find tasks that can be successfully combined.

One of the best opportunities to multitask is while doing your laundry. Laundry takes up a lot of your time and there is no way to avoid it. So, while your clothes are in the washer or dryer do some reading, get ahead on an assignment, or review the notes you took in class that day. If you are already caught up on your studies or the noise of the machines distracts you, use laundry time to write your family a letter, fill out birthday cards for friends, or plan your holiday shopping list.

Whenever you find yourself waiting for something, this might also be a good opportunity to combine tasks. Whether you are waiting to see a doctor, waiting in a long line at the grocery store, or waiting for a bus or train, you can always use the time to your advantage. If you know you will have to endure a waiting period at some point in the day, carry some note cards or a book with you. Even if you only get through a few cards or a few pages, the wait will go by quicker and you'll be closer to accomplishing your task.

Identify small weekly tasks and try to accomplish them while doing other things. For example, you cannot brush your teeth while you talk on the phone, but you can talk on the phone while you fold laundry. Small tasks are often the best candidates for combination.

Many students try to study while watching television. While this seems like a good way to multitask, it's actually counterproductive. You will not pay full attention to the material you're trying to learn because you will be distracted by what's going on in the television show. Studying should usually be done in a quiet area with minimal distractions, such as the library, a computer lab, or in your room with the door closed. Every student studies differently, however, so determine what works best for you and stick to it.

There are several tasks you can accomplish while watching television. Use that time to fold or iron laundry, prepare a to-do list for the following day, or write letters to friends from home.

## *Planners and Calendars*

There are enough planners, calendar systems, and other time management aids to make a student's head spin. You can literally spend hundreds of dollars on time management computer software or on books about time management. However, as a student, you will not need or be able to afford such materials. Some students choose to keep track of their time using basic student planners while others prefer to jot notes on wall calendars. Be sure to consider all of your options before selecting your own time management strategy.

Office supply stores and your college bookstore sell an array of planners that could be helpful to you. Initially, the variety may seem overwhelming; daily, weekly, monthly, pocket size, desktop, portfolio, and wall-mounted are among the available options. Just look closely at each style and consider how you want to manage your time. A pocket-size planner, for example, is handy to carry with you, but it does not offer a lot of space to write your plans. Most students choose notebook-size planners that they can take to class along with other books. These planners make it easy to write down the dates of upcoming exams and deadlines as soon as you get the information.

**ALERT!**

Some college students approach time management overconfidently, thinking that they can keep track of everything in their heads. However, just as it is difficult for a waiter to remember several dinner and drink orders without writing them down, most students cannot succeed in college without documenting assignments, appointments, and other plans.

Your word processing program may provide an alternative to purchasing a planner. It probably has a calendar template you can customize and then print out. You can then post a copy over your desk and put one in your notebook. And if you make a mistake or need to change something about the schedule you've made, you can simply reopen the file, make the adjustment, and print another copy. But if your word processing program does not have a template for a calendar or planner, or the template does not suit your needs, you can use another computer program to create your own. This strategy will allow you to decide how large or small to make the calendar, how many time increments to include, and which fonts and colors work best.

It's important to make your planner visually effective, whether it is a homemade calendar or a store-bought planner. To achieve this, you may want to color-code your schedule or use a highlighter to draw attention to important points. Other ways to personalize your calendar include marking important days with stickers or adhesive tabs, adding countdowns to upcoming holidays or exciting events, or adding photos of friends and family. No matter how you create or customize your planner, the important thing is that you have one, keep it updated, and reference it often.

Your college will provide you with a calendar of each semester or the entire academic year. This calendar may include dates of final exam periods, seasonal and holiday breaks, and other major events at the college, such as Homecoming weekend. If you have chosen to use a planner to manage your time, be sure to mark it with these important college dates right away.

Some students use Personal Digital Assistants (PDAs), which are essentially hand-held computers that store information, such as schedules and address books. Most PDAs offer various functions, including phone, camera, e-mail, and music capabilities. The downside to having all of these extra features is that you may lose sight of what functions you actually need. If you purchase a PDA make sure it serves your basic needs and can easily be made compatible with your computer. You also need to find one that is durable; your PDA will often be tossed into your backpack, and your backpack might then be tossed onto the floor. One big advantage of most PDAs is the alarm feature. This function can be used to wake you up, remind you about an upcoming meeting or appointment, or alert you to the approach of a deadline.

## Cramming Warning

All-night cramming sessions seem to be a rite of passage among college students. Every year students use this method when studying for final exams, but in truth, this strategy is usually far from effective. Losing a full night's sleep will leave you lethargic and unfocused in the morning. When you arrive for your exam you may have trouble keeping your eyes open, focusing on the page in front of you, or writing coherently. As a rule, don't rely upon cramming. But if your time management strategy has gone awry and you need to fit a lot of studying into a short period of time, try to at least get a few hours of sleep and eat breakfast before your test.

In most cases, cramming can be (and should be) avoided. If you are using a planner, calendar, PDA, or other time management system but are still finding the need to cram for tests, ask your RA, academic advisor, or health center staff for guidance. The problem may be that you cannot focus on your studies because your residence hall is too noisy or your neighbors are being inconsiderate during exam periods. If this is the case, your RA can seize control over the situation. If you have simply overloaded your schedule and don't have time to complete your assignments and study for tests, your academic advisor should be able to offer assistance. And if frequent headaches interrupt your study time, causing you to put it off until the last minute, you may need reading glasses or some kind of medication. Your health center staff may be able to identify such a problem and suggest a solution. Whatever your trouble, you won't have to work through it alone. Ask for help when needed and heed the advice you receive.

## Chapter 12

# New Friends and Activities

Though your priority at college is to succeed in your academic pursuits, your life will certainly extend beyond the classroom. In addition to getting to know other students, you want to meet others on campus and get involved in a variety of activities. While the range of possibilities may be daunting, you are very fortunate to have so many opportunities at your fingertips. Take your time deciding which commitments to make, try a variety of new things, and be sure to balance study time with fun.

# Where to Meet People

After the initial excitement of move-in day and your first few classes has died down, you will probably want to get involved in college activities and meet some new people. But since this is your first time at college, you probably won't know where to go or who to speak with to locate the social scene. Fortunately, social opportunities abound on college campuses, and the more effort you put into finding these opportunities, the more choices you will have.

## Your Room

The first place to start socializing is in your own room. Your roommate is the first person you have the chance to form a relationship with. She may or may not end up being your lifelong best friend, but she is the person you will see most often during your first semester of college. Not only is she valuable as a friend in her own right, she will soon be meeting new people whom she can introduce you to.

Judge people gently and give new people a second or third chance to make a good impression. Remember that most new students are nervous and will try very hard to make friends. If people around you seem overzealous or say the wrong things, be patient with them. You may find yourself acting similarly soon enough.

Your room is also a place of opportunity by virtue of the people you attract to it. Early in the semester when you are hanging out or studying in your room, keep the door propped open. The music you are playing or the way you have decorated your room may attract people with similar tastes. One or two people walking down the hall may see your open door and take a moment to see how you have set up your room. If you say hello and invite them in, you can begin to get to know each other. This will give you the chance to talk about the things in your room that are special to you, such as family photos, posters or paintings, or a favorite book or movie. Of course, there will be times to keep your room door closed, such as when you are sleeping or are on the phone with your family. Otherwise, keeping your door ajar is an easy way to potentially meet new people.

## *Your Residence Hall*

Just outside of your room is a building full of new and diverse people. Make a point to walk up and down the hallways of your building and look for rooms with open doors. Walk by these rooms slowly and look for an opportunity to start a conversation with the people you see. They may have decorated or arranged their rooms differently than yours, so something intriguing may catch your eye. You will also hear music or see decorations that match your interests. When you see a person sitting in a room make eye contact with him, smile, and say hello. If he invites you in, take a few minutes to stop and talk to him. You may find that those few minutes turn into a couple of hours and, before you know it, you could be making plans to have lunch with this new acquaintance.

**QUESTION?**

**What if you are too shy to approach other people?**
Even if you have trouble initiating conversations, you still need to be out and about, giving other people the chance to approach you. If you experience a lull in a conversation, ask the others about their residence halls, homes, or hobbies. People enjoy a chance to talk about themselves, and this will give you insight into their personalities.

Besides individual rooms, there are a couple of other places in your residence hall where you can meet new friends. Your residence hall will likely have a lounge—a room or open space with several couches, a TV, or other entertainment equipment. As the semester progresses, your RA will probably plan events to take place in the lounge, or you and your friends can use it as a place to hang out. Aside from the lounge, your residence hall may have a service desk located in a central area of the building. Generally, the service desk is a place where students can seek help with specific problems, borrow movies, collect mail, or buy stamps. If you make a point to visit your service desk often, you will meet other people borrowing movies who may invite you to join them. Or, if your RA is working at the service desk, you can use your visit as an opportunity to get to know her better.

## *Your Campus*

Your room and residence hall are a good place to start meeting and greeting new people, but don't forget that there is a big campus surrounding you. Your campus is full of fun and interesting people, so you should make a point to leave your room and explore this new community. Start with the obvious places, such as the cafeteria and student center. During the first few weeks of classes new students will usually be a little timid and won't quite know the routine of the campus. So, when you find yourself in the cafeteria with a tray full of food, look for a table where one or two people are sitting alone. Confidently approach these people and ask if you can join them. Notice the books they are carrying, the food they have selected, or the clothing that they are wearing. These details may make great conversation-starters. Even if you came to the cafeteria with your roommate, suggest to her that you sit with others instead of by yourselves.

## QUESTION?

**How do you initiate conversation with a total stranger?**
The key to starting up a conversation with a student you don't know is noticing familiar details. If you see someone wearing a sweatshirt with the name of your favorite football team on it, go over and say hello. You might discover that this fellow sports fan will also be in your biology class the following week.

There are a variety of places in the student center to meet new people. Waiting in line or browsing at the bookstore gives you a chance to initiate casual conversation with those around you. While this may not result in deep friendships, you may soon encounter these people again. You may discover them sitting alone in the cafeteria the next day, right next to you in a class later in the week, or living nearby in your residence hall. If there are people around you while you wait in line for coffee or read flyers on a bulletin board, don't be afraid to say hello to them. These are among the many opportunities to strike up conversations with new people. You don't have to linger for long; just a brief exchange can lay the groundwork for future conversations.

Many organizations will sponsor educational as well as social events, sometimes combining the two. You may have the opportunity to see a political debate, learn about holidays such as Kwanzaa or Passover, or hear a new form of music. These events are not only opportunities to meet new people, but they will also provide you with interesting anecdotes to share with friends and family.

While running into people at the bookstore may be easy, it is not necessarily the best way to start friendships. If you want to meet a larger or more diverse group of people, you should look for more organized opportunities. Clubs and organizations, which are discussed later in this chapter, offer opportunities for you to meet and socialize with people who have interests similar to your own. Your college will also sponsor a wide variety of activities to help you escape from your room and take a break from your studies. Virtually every college sponsors movie showings allowing you to see popular movies for free or at a small cost. This is a good opportunity to gather a few casual acquaintances and express similar interests. There will also be comedy acts, concerts, and other shows coming to campus on a regular basis. Take advantage of these opportunities by gathering a group to go with you or, at the very least, attending on your own and trying to meet new people.

Your college will also probably sponsor some late night activities, such as dances, open mic events, or mini-carnivals. It is best if you can go to these events with a small group of other students, but if nobody in your hall is interested, you should still attend by yourself. You will probably find someone else who is at the event alone and with whom you can strike up a conversation. You can also join an existing group, invite new people into your group, or move from group to group as the event wears on. The important thing is to be yourself and find others whom you enjoy spending time with. If you make the effort to talk to other people, they will generally receive you warmly, and you will again lay the foundation for future conversations. You will see these people in the cafeteria and be able to join them for meals, or see them walking across campus and accompany them to a common destination. Don't be disappointed if you don't meet your best friend within your first week of college. Eventually, genuine friendships will develop naturally.

Many clubs and organizations will host social events throughout the semester. These events may take place somewhere on campus or at a local cafe or restaurant. While the organization is sponsoring the event to attract new members or otherwise win the support of students, this represents an opportunity for you to get out of your room, have fun, and get to know new people. Whether this is a dance, a performance, or a student-faculty mixer, the event will allow you to find people with whom you have something in common.

## The Activities Fair

There are many different ways to learn about what activities are available to you on your college campus. You can simply read the flyers you see hanging up in the cafeteria, library, or residence halls. You can also read your college newspaper to learn about upcoming events and club meetings. But probably the best way to discover campus activities is to attend your college's activities fair. Usually, colleges hold an activities fair at least once per semester to advertise the clubs, organizations, and athletic teams available to students. This event will consist of representatives from each group educating students about their causes. You can approach the tables of the groups that interest you and receive information about their meeting times, long-range goals, and membership requirements.

Go to the activities fair with your roommate and a few friends from your residence hall. Take the time to walk around and see everything before you start to sign up with groups. Ask a lot of questions and find out what each group stands for, what is included in the membership, and what kinds of events the group sponsors. After you have seen all of the organizations that are available go back and sign up with those you find most appealing.

Consider the activities you participated in during high school, but also learn about new opportunities—things that were not available to you before but that you find interesting.

Many groups will have sign-up sheets where you can write your name and e-mail address. If you choose to sign up with a group, be sure to ask what you are signing up for. Are you volunteering to organize an event for the organization, promising to attend the group's next meeting, or simply requesting more information? Talk to the representatives and get as many details as possible. It might help to have a notebook and pen with you so you can jot down notes.

In addition to highlighting clubs and organizations, an activities fair will usually include free food and many groups will give away small items. Even if you don't end up joining a group, you will certainly leave the event with some snacks and a few free pens or key chains. You may also encounter booths for local merchants offering coupons or product samples.

Even if you don't end up joining any of the groups you see advertised at the activities fair, you can still use the opportunity to meet some fellow students—particularly upperclassmen. As a freshman, friendships with sophomores, juniors, and seniors can be very helpful. These knowledgeable students can help you get around campus, guide your class choices, and eventually help you find internships and jobs.

## How to Choose

The key to participating in college activities is being able to make a meaningful contribution. You must have enough time and energy to give to an activity, as well as to maintain your studies. So, as the semester progresses keep track of how much you are able to give to each activity. If you are a member of eight clubs and barely have time to attend the meetings, you aren't being a productive member. Not only are you doing a disservice to each club, you are not benefiting yourself at all. Conversely, if you are a member of two organizations and still have a lot of free time you might consider doing other things on campus. While you don't need to fill every waking minute of your day you should find ways to contribute to causes you care about, meet new people, and have fun—outside of the classroom. Remember what you learned about time management in the last chapter and apply it not only to your studies, but also to your activities.

If you find you're having trouble making time for meals, if you're extremely overtired, or if you don't have time for basic responsibilities like laundry and studying, you're probably overextending yourself. One or two extracurricular activities are plenty. Too many more will drastically limit your free time and could even become detrimental to your health.

It is important for you to balance your schoolwork with involvement in clubs and organizations. These experiences will look good on your resume, help you meet new people, and possibly teach you invaluable leadership, citizenship, and time management skills. Sometimes your classes may seem overwhelming and you will have trouble finding the time for anything else. But even if you have to miss a few meetings, sticking with the commitment you made will be beneficial in the end. If you have to cut down on activities, maintain the few that you find most enjoyable and think of them as chances to escape from your studies for a while.

Committing to a group is an important decision. In doing this you will have to accept even the tedious aspects of membership. If you only volunteer to help out with fun group events, like car washes, and ignore the less exciting obligations, like photocopying flyers, you may instill resentment in your fellow group members.

## *Local Attractions*

Among the most overlooked assets of any college are the local attractions. From historical parks and natural resources to city shops and quaint cafes, your campus is surrounded by opportunities for you to get out and try new things. If your RA does not have local attractions listed on a bulletin board, ask him what is available in the area. Also, reference your student handbook and other materials that were given to you during orientation. You can often find out a lot about the area through your college's Web site. Almost every college Web site has a section for students and another for parents. One or both of these sections will have information about local attractions, and perhaps even recommendations for day trips. You will also find links to the local chamber of commerce and perhaps the visitor's bureau. These sites will be rich with information about things to do on a free afternoon or for a weekend.

Whether you have a car or not, you should watch for college-sponsored trips to regional attractions. Your student activities office or student organizations will probably sponsor trips to museums, historical landmarks, and other attractions that are outside of the local area. These events are usually free for students or include a nominal fee to help cover the cost of a bus.

Early in your college career, you should try to get away from campus and explore the area around you. This will give you a chance to deepen friendships with people from your floor or others that you have met on campus, and when you return to your residence hall you will be an expert about available resources and can advise other interested students. This is also helpful if you plan to have family or friends visit from home. For example, if you have explored a little bit you can bypass the chains and take your family to a charming local restaurant for a nice meal. Or you can take your friends from home to a historic theater to see a play or to a nearby lake for a swim on a warm afternoon.

## A Relationship with Your RA

Too often RAs are stereotyped as cruel enforcers of college policy. Though they do have the unpleasant responsibility of keeping order in raucous residence halls, RAs are just students doing their best to complete requirements and graduate with degrees. In fact, most RAs take the job so that they can help new students adjust to college life; they aren't trying to ruin anyone's fun. A big part of an RA's job is organizing activities and programs for the residents on her floor or in her building. Some of these programs will be educational in nature, but they can also be very interesting and exciting. Your RA might arrange for a singer to put on a show in your hall, or invite a martial arts expert to teach you and your peers some new moves.

**QUESTION?**

**What does it take to be an RA?**
RAs are usually students with at least one semester of college under their belts. The job requires patience, a passion for working with people, and the fortitude to remain confident in the face of criticism. The benefits include a stipend or a discount on tuition or room and board for their services, and they often get residence hall rooms to themselves.

Your RA will work hard to put up bulletin boards to inform and entertain you, be available when you are struggling, mediate conflicts on the floor, and help you socialize. The school may even give the RA a budget for planning programs. This is where you come in. Don't be afraid to offer suggestions to your RA—in fact, she will probably appreciate your insight. You should talk to your RA about activities that you would enjoy, or ask your RA about campus programs that you have heard about. She will probably work that much harder to meet your needs because you have expressed an interest in her efforts. Sometimes your RA will even ask you to help her organize a program you suggest. This is a way for you to get involved and gain more control over your life. And if you think that you may want to be an RA in the future, working with your own RA will give you insight into the position.

Though your RA is certainly there to be your friend and guide, he is also there to enforce residence hall rules and college regulations. Most RAs are required to report incidences of alcohol consumption, property destruction, and excessive noise on their floors. Just because you have become friends with your RA it doesn't mean that he won't report you if you break one of the rules. Don't take advantage of your RA, and don't put him in a position that will be uncomfortable for either of you. Be respectful of your peers, your RA, and your building, and you will get along fine.

## Avoiding the Extremes

When it comes to committing to clubs, participating in activities, and making friends, some students do too much and others do too little. You don't want to overschedule your time and become stressed out, but you do need to avoid isolation and travel out of your comfort zone. Pursue a certain level of social involvement and work hard to excel in your classes, but don't allow yourself to fall to the extremes.

A big mistake many new college students make is just sitting in their rooms. Some students stay in their rooms waiting for friends to come find them, convinced that it will happen on its own. Other students remain in their rooms because they feel shy or are uncertain about how to approach other people. For the first few weeks of the semester, you should try to spend as little time as possible in your room. Walk down your residence hall corridor and look into other rooms where doors are propped open. If you see a student sitting alone in a room knock lightly, say hello, and introduce yourself. If nothing else, get out and walk around campus. Look for groups of new students who are hanging out together and join them. Whatever you do, don't isolate yourself. Most students form friendships within the first couple of months of college, and it is much harder to join existing groups than it is to meet new people one on one.

On the other end of the spectrum are students who try to do everything during the first semester. It is important to be active on campus, but it is easy to overdo things. Students who are overinvolved too early in their college careers, or students who work too much on the social part of college life, tend to be struggling academically at the end of the first semester. Keep in mind that you have several years of college to do everything that you want to do. Pace yourself and build your involvement in activities slowly. Stick with the three or four activities that are the most fun for you, spend time making new friends, and focus a lot of your energy on your schoolwork. After your first semester, you will have a good idea of how much you can do outside of class and will be able to increase your involvement if there is free time in your schedule.

Many new college students view the college years as a chance to start over, to be who they really are, and to escape the perceptions other students had about them in high school. This is true. However, this thought process leads some students to try changing themselves to impress others. The best piece of advice you have received from family and friends is to be yourself. Your efforts to be someone other than your true self will fail. In the meantime, other students who recognize your dishonesty will be reluctant to befriend you. Soon you will feel out of place and under pressure to maintain the false identity. If you act naturally and allow yourself to make mistakes, you will find genuine friends and a place for yourself within the first month or two of college.

If you routinely feel uncomfortable in new situations or are struggling with the conflict between being yourself and trying new things, a visit to your college counseling center is in order. Most likely just a few visits will help you sort out what you are experiencing and develop strategies for managing these feelings and your new experiences.

A new environment with new people sometimes includes uncomfortable situations. Some discomfort is normal and healthy, and you will learn valuable skills by working through unfamiliar circumstances. But at some point, you might be in an uncomfortable situation where you know something is wrong. Your friends may be trying to persuade you to do something you don't want to do, or you may feel that your personal security is being violated. These can be difficult times, but they are also the times when you have the opportunity to let your true character shine.

If you are with a group of new friends and they are doing something questionable, ask yourself a few questions. Are you willing to tell your family about what you're doing? Is the situation potentially dangerous? Would you do this if your new friends were not there to egg you on? Generally, you should trust your instincts in these situations; if you feel uncomfortable you should probably remove yourself from the activity. If you cannot think of a good excuse to leave the group, you can always tell the others that you have to use the bathroom. This will give you time to get out of the situation and think for a few minutes. Never sacrifice your personal values to impress others. Sincere friends will come along in time.

**Chapter 13**

# Athletics

Athletics are a major part of almost any college. Athletics programs help the school recruit students, build school spirit, help students develop and learn while at college, promote fundraising for the school, and keep alumni connected with the institution. Athletics can be a lot of fun, whether you're a participant or a spectator. You can choose to become a part of a varsity sports team, play an intramural sport for fun, or simply work out at the gym to keep in shape.

## *Varsity Level*

If you choose to participate in varsity athletics, you must navigate a complex system. Your high school coach may be able to help you through this process, but ultimately it is up to you to find the situation that is best for you. The first issue you must contend with is motivation. Do you want to participate in varsity athletics for the scholarship money, for the challenge this involvement presents, or for the opportunity to move through college athletics and become a professional athlete? If you're striving for the latter, then be warned: Very few college athletes go on to have professional athletic careers. You can dedicate yourself to your sport, do everything your college coaches tell you to do, and still never get the chance you're hoping for. In the meantime, if you don't pay attention to your academics, you could lose your opportunity to get a degree and find yourself back at square one.

**ALERT!**

Many student-athletes eventually forget that "student" is their primary role. Don't take your academic obligations lightly or neglect them in favor of athletic pursuits. There are a lot of resources available to you, but it is ultimately up to you to make use of them. You can be successful—in every part of your life—if you maintain balance, focus, and motivation.

If an athletics scholarship allows you to attend a good college and earn a degree, be aware of the hard work you have ahead of you. Institutions that offer athletics scholarships often treat your sport like a job—you must fulfill your responsibility to your team in order to receive money toward your education. To uphold these obligations, you will have to forego many social opportunities and manage your time with expert skill. However, you will receive a good education at a significantly reduced price and you will enjoy the other benefits of intercollegiate athletics.

If you are motivated by the extra challenge athletics participation will give you, then you have several options to choose from. You can select any level of athletic competition and have total control over the balance between athletics and the rest of your college life. However, if you do make a commitment to a team, you should not take it less seriously than if you were playing the sport to uphold a scholarship. Choose only a level of competition you can handle, without losing sight of your academic goals.

In order to compete at an NCAA Division I school you must have superior athletic ability, a lot of self-confidence, a solid academic record, and a strategy for getting noticed by college scouts. If you are missing any of these items, it will be difficult for you to become part of a highly competitive Division I team. You, your family, and your high school coaches should sit down together and plan how to attract the attention of college scouts. You should also develop a list of things that you are looking for in a school, coach, and team.

If a team does not recruit you, you can still compete for a spot and possibly a scholarship. Here are some tips, if you decide to do this:

- Notify the head coach at your chosen college of your intent to try out for the team
- Learn the dates and times for open tryouts
- Have a complete physical through your primary care physician, and find out if the team requires any additional medical documentation
- Adhere to the summer training regimen prescribed for athletes in this sport

Always keep in mind that you are not guaranteed a spot on the team just because you have worked hard and "earned" it, in your opinion. College athletic programs tend to be highly selective, and even if you were the best player in your high school, you may not yet have the skill to play for a college team. If you don't get a spot on your first try, don't give up. Prepare yourself further the following year and try again. Even if you never get a spot on the team the coach will notice your persistence and possibly suggest an alternative. You could use your knowledge of the sport to write a sports column in the college newspaper, start your own intramural team, or even coach at a nearby high school.

Participation below the NCAA Division I level may be less stressful, but it is no less important. You again need to have a clear idea of what type of experience you are looking for, and be certain that questions about academics are the first you pose to coaches who come to recruit you. At any level you need to expect that participating in intercollegiate athletics constitutes a year-round commitment. Even out of season, you will likely have a training regimen to maintain, and your coach will likely advise you on how to keep in shape throughout the summer.

College courses are more difficult and faster paced than those you took in high school. When you couple these increased academic demands with the time and energy needed to participate in intercollegiate athletics, you are likely to struggle a bit. However, there will be several resources available to help you. Often coaches or team captains will set up study groups for team members. Larger schools may have staff or resource centers available to help athletes manage their academic challenges. Look for and take advantage of these resources. Also, let your professors know that you are an athlete and therefore may miss some classes when traveling to other schools for competitions. You will still have to complete all work on time, but if your professor knows why you are absent you will generally not be penalized.

Scholarships aren't just for football and basketball players. Colleges that offer athletic scholarships have them for many sports. If golf or tennis has been your passion then ask your college about scholarships in those areas. And even if you cannot get a full scholarship, partial scholarships can still cover a significant portion of your tuition.

It is easy to fall into a lifestyle that consists only of academics and athletics. Though it may be hard work at first it is important that you find friends outside of athletics. You are going to see your teammates every day and spend a lot of time with them. Meeting a more diverse group of people will be more fun for you and help you maintain a balanced and healthy lifestyle. Don't be discouraged if this is difficult initially; your adjustment to college life may be a bit more challenging than it is for students who choose not to participate in intercollegiate athletics. However, your hard work will prove beneficial well beyond your college years.

# *Intramurals*

Every college offers some sort of intramural sports program, and some even set up leagues for athletes of varying abilities. Many students participate in intramural sports for the fun of playing, for the camaraderie of being on a team, or simply for the excitement of competition. The range of intramural sports includes team-oriented competition, such as basketball, football, and volleyball, as well as individual or pair sports, such as tennis and racquetball.

Decide in advance how competitive you want to be in your intramural sport. If you just want to have fun, then avoid the leagues that are highly competitive. Intramural basketball, for example, is sometimes broken down into "A" and "B" leagues to separate people by skill level and competitiveness. Also, assemble teammates who take the same approach you do.

Intramurals are a great opportunity for you to have a lot of fun with new friends and get some good exercise in the process. You will see advertisements for intramural sports programs in your school newspaper or on flyers posted around campus. When you see one that interests you, gather people from your residence hall and register a team. If you are feeling competitive, recruit those people who you know to be good athletes. If you just want to have fun pick people who you enjoy spending time with and who will not take the competition too seriously. Also, you will get the opportunity to name your team. This may seem silly, but take a little extra time to brainstorm about fun team names as a group. You may come up with a name that is intimidating, funny, or one that incorporates the first letters of all your teammates' names. You and your teammates may even decide to make your own T-shirts or jerseys to wear in competition.

If you don't want to start your own team or can't find anybody who is interested in a particular sport check with the intramural office—probably located somewhere in the athletics department. Often this office will have a sign-up sheet for people who are interested in playing but don't have a team.

Another group needing one or two more players may contact you and invite you to join them. You will still get the opportunity to play and have fun, as well as meet new people.

Intramurals are a year-round occurrence though the sports will vary by season. If you want to spend your first semester getting used to your academic challenges and new freedom, don't feel like you are missing out on participating in intramurals. Another season will be starting soon, and the key is to take advantage of the opportunity only when you are ready.

## Clubs

Many colleges have club sports available, either to meet a special interest or to fill a gap where an intercollegiate team is not available. Sports clubs often compete with other colleges and sometimes with community groups. Examples of club sports might include fencing, crew, and rugby. These clubs give you the opportunity to play a sport you love or learn a sport that is new to you. The one drawback to club sports is that colleges often don't fund them. In these cases, club members have to work hard to organize fundraisers and collect money to keep their sports going.

**ALERT!**

Club sports often involve special equipment. Items such as uniforms are easily stored, but larger equipment can be difficult to obtain and keep secure. Explore funding options with your student government, student activities office, and athletics office. You might also arrange for storage by working with the athletics office or maintenance department.

Club sports are less time-consuming than other athletic endeavors, and you can easily miss a practice or even a competition if your academic or work commitments are particularly demanding at a certain point. You can also leave a club sport if you find it just isn't working out. However, it's worth it to stick with a club sport for a while. Too many students quit early because they aren't doing as well as they hoped or they don't seem to be fitting in.

You should give yourself at least half a semester to truly evaluate your experience with a club.

You may come to college with a passion for a particular sport, only to find that there is not an existing team or the team has been disbanded for budgetary or other reasons. Don't let this discourage you. If you can find a group of other students who are also interested in your sport then you can start your own club. Place an ad in your school newspaper or post flyers around campus announcing an organizational meeting. Once you have a committed handful of people approach your student activities or athletics office and find out what you need to do to be recognized as a club sport. Often you will be able to organize a group and receive some funding to help support your interest. You will also be able to list this accomplishment on your resume and discuss your initiative when you interview for jobs.

## Physical Education Classes

Just as in high school you may find that your college curriculum includes a physical education component. But rather than groan at the thought of taking yet another gym class, look for the opportunity to try something new or learn more about a familiar sport. Colleges offer a much broader range of physical education classes that will fulfill the requirement. They also have larger budgets for equipment, so you may be able to experiment with a sport you wouldn't otherwise have the chance to try.

A good example of a specialized gym class you might consider is tai-kwan-do, or another martial art. Some colleges offer students the chance to take golf or archery classes. Review your options and choose something that interests you. Taking a physical education class could fill your core requirement, inspire you to continue with the activity after your class ends, and provide a fun diversion from your other classes. You may learn some valuable stress-relief techniques or find out that you have a real talent for this type of activity.

You may even have the opportunity to participate in seasonal sports classes. Some colleges offer classes such as skiing or snowshoeing during the winter months. Colleges located in warmer climates might teach surfing or outdoor rock climbing. Look at your college bulletin to see if such classes are listed there. If so, inquire with your registrar's office about when those classes will be offered next. Don't rush to fill your requirement and simply take the first class that comes to your attention. It is worth waiting a semester or a year for the opportunity to take a class that is interesting and potentially valuable to you.

If you have a particular athletic skill you may be able to instruct one of these classes for academic credit or as a work-study job. If this sounds interesting to you approach your physical education department and find out what kinds of assistance are needed. You could teach an aerobics class, provide weight training instruction, or help fellow students with their golf swing.

Even if your curriculum does not include a physical education requirement, you may still want to consider taking one of these classes. If you have some flexibility in your schedule, a physical education class could balance out the stress of other more formal courses. It is also a great opportunity to meet other students in a unique setting. Occasionally, professors will take these classes as well, or instruct them, even if the activity is outside of their academic specialty. For example, your biology professor might have a personal enthusiasm for mountain biking and teach such a class one semester each year. Seeing your professor in a new light and getting to know him better outside of the classroom can only help you in your academic career.

## Going Solo

You don't need a team, organization, or class to enjoy athletics at college. There are a plethora of activities you can do on your own or with a few friends. Your campus will have an athletic facility that is open to students year-round, and it is in your best interest to take advantage of that opportunity. Moreover, many colleges have equipment you can borrow or rent. You don't necessarily have to bring your basketball or tennis racket to college in order to enjoy these activities casually. Just take your I.D. to the gym and sign out the equipment you want to use for the day. Many colleges will also assign you a locker in the gym where you can leave your athletic gear, clean clothes, or water bottle. You may even find that your college offers a towel service—they give you a towel to use during your workout that you must return before you leave the gym.

If you're interested in playing basketball but don't want to join a pre-existing team, you should just shoot baskets on your own in the gym. Though it may take some time, others may see you and ask if you would like to play one-on-one, or participate in a tournament they have arranged. You may also encounter a couple of people looking for a pick-up game. Don't be shy if others express interest in playing with you. This is a great opportunity to meet friends who share your interest.

Many students also swim for exercise or for fun while at college. Swimming is very good exercise and is usually available year-round on campus. In addition, the only equipment you need is a swimsuit and perhaps some goggles, both of which take up virtually no space in your room. But keep in mind that if you are only swimming recreationally, you will have to visit the pool around the swim team's practice schedule. Remember also to learn the school's rules regarding swimming. Do they only allow swimmers to use the pool when a lifeguard is on duty? Do you have to pass a swimming test before you can use the pool? Contact your college's athletic department with such questions.

**QUESTION?**

**How do you find other students to participate in these sports?**
Word of mouth is usually your best option; ask friends and other students in your hall if they are interested. You can also ask your RA to help you organize a team or event. And consider posting flyers around your residence hall or campus if you want to attract a more diverse group.

Bicycles are also helpful to have on college campuses. Though a bike is bulky and will likely not fit in your residence hall room, your college will have bike racks and perhaps an interior storage room available to you. The extra effort it takes getting a bike to and from campus is well worth it; biking is a lot of fun and is very good exercise. From a practical standpoint, a bike can get you across campus quickly and easily, even in the winter. Or if you have a job somewhere in town, you can use a bike to get there instead of a car. You may also find a biking club on campus, either for street riding or mountain biking. However, it is imperative that you secure your bike when it is not in use. Bikes are easy targets for thieves, so be sure to invest in a bike lock and use it consistently.

## Spectator Sports

Most colleges have a full range of intercollegiate teams, so you can attend sports competitions year-round. At larger schools, more popular sports, like football and basketball, may attract fans from all over the area. Smaller sports will also attract a group of fans. While being a spectator does not provide you with much exercise, it is a great way to show school spirit, to have fun with friends, and to cheer your school's team on to victory.

Buying merchandise with your team's name on it is another way to show support for your college sports. Sometimes the profits of these sales will go directly to the team for new equipment. Also, keep an eye out for team fundraising events. Just buying a cookie or a bookmark from a college team could help them afford new uniforms for the next season.

At smaller schools, you will still find intense intercollegiate rivalries. You are also likely to have free admission for every contest. But the biggest advantage is that you are likely to know one or two of the athletes representing your school. Perhaps the star quarterback was in your English class your first semester or the starting forward on the basketball team was your freshman year roommate. This can personalize an event for you, and your support will mean a lot to your athlete friends. Another advantage of a small college athletic program is the opportunity for good seats. You will be able to walk in just before the game begins and still get an excellent seat in perfect view of all the action.

Attending sporting events is more than just an opportunity for you to express school spirit or support your friends. A soccer or football game offers a chance to get out of your residence hall and away from your studies for a few hours. If the weather is nice, a football game is a great outdoor event. And if the weather is cold or rainy, a basketball game could be a great way to get out of your comfort zone while still being involved on campus. By attending sporting events you may also end up in some photos featured in a local newspaper, on the campus Web site, or in the college yearbook. Whatever your motivation, take advantage of these opportunities and support your teams.

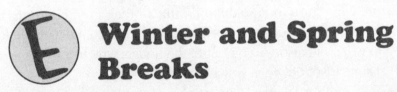

*Chapter 14*

# Winter and Spring Breaks

When you find yourself back at home for winter break, you may be eager to return to college where you have more independence and friends all around you. These feelings are natural and you will learn how to deal with them in time. Also, deciding what to do during your first spring break can be difficult. You will want to make the most of the experience without spending too much money. In either case, a bit of planning can lead to a fun and rewarding break experience.

# *Returning to Your Old Job*

Returning to the job you had in high school may seem like a step backward. Though only a few months will have passed, you may dread returning to your low-paying job where you might have awkward run-ins with old acquaintances. Still, try your best to be positive about the situation. The opportunity to return to an old job during a break from college is a valuable one—you can earn some needed money and reunite with old friends. Going to work will also get you out of the house, which you might want to do if tension arises between you and your family.

During a fall or Thanksgiving break, whether you go home or not, get in touch with your former employer and make arrangements to work again during winter break. Remember to point out that you are experienced in the job and offer to work flexible hours. During the holiday rush, your experience will certainly be an asset, and since you will likely be able to work daytime hours even after high school students have returned to school you may be more marketable as a seasonal employee. If your former employer does not need help during your winter break you could try finding work through a temp agency. These companies specialize in finding work for students, people who are between jobs, and those in other special situations. If this option doesn't work, you could try babysitting or shoveling snow for neighbors. These activities may not yield large profits, but the money will be untaxed and your neighbors will appreciate your services.

If you do return to a previous employer, it may be an opportunity to gain more experience. Ask for more responsibility and perhaps a higher wage. Not only do you have the chance to earn more money, you can gain experience that will serve you well in the future. If you can be placed in charge of new employees, manage a shift, or handle other responsibilities you can add these things to your resume. This may help when applying for internships, jobs on campus, or employment after college. Sell yourself to your employer. What have you learned while at college? Why will you be a better employee now? Why should she give you greater responsibility? Be confident in your abilities and your potential.

If you do not need or cannot find a job while you are home for winter break, you still need to do something to fill your time. In addition to the suggestions listed later in this chapter, you might consider shadowing a professional in your desired career field. You could also volunteer at a community service organization, such as an animal shelter or soup kitchen. These experiences can help you in many ways. If you shadow a professional, you will gain good experience and a valuable reference for future jobs or internships. And if you contribute to your community through volunteer work, you will be doing something fulfilling and worthwhile—as opposed to sleeping in every day and watching a lot of television.

**ALERT!**

If you return to an old job during a college break, be prepared to find an entirely new staff working there. It's possible that one of your friends will still be working, but many of them may have found other jobs or gone to college like you. If this is the case, be patient with less experienced employees and remember that you are only working there temporarily.

Since spring break periods are rarely more than a week long, it is harder to find good employment during this time. For such a short break, you are better off pursuing another opportunity. Unless you really need the money, you will probably want to spend your spring break on vacation, visiting friends, or spending time with family. If you need to gain some income during your spring break, ask your neighbors if they need help with any odd jobs. Many people choose to paint their homes in the springtime, and several of your neighbors will surely need help with landscaping chores.

## Visiting New Friends

If you will not be working and are looking for ways to fill the time during winter or spring break, you should consider taking a trip to visit some of your college friends. If you have friends who live in a different part of the country, this is a wonderful opportunity to see places you have never visited. You might also have the opportunity to try new experiences. For example, if you are from the south consider visiting a friend who lives up north. You could try skiing, ice-skating, snowmobiling, or snowshoeing for the first time.

Although your family will probably want you to spend your entire break at home, you will likely prefer to continue exercising the independent life-style that you have at college. You should not neglect your family, so you could spend some time with them and some time traveling elsewhere. Visiting your new friends will allow you to maintain your independence while furthering your life experience. You can strengthen a new friendship, travel to a new place, and make great memories. When visiting friends at their homes, always be polite and express your appreciation for the hospitality you receive.

Before inviting friends to your home or heading out to visit a friend at her home, be sure to talk to your family about your plans. Your family may have certain expectations for your break, such as visiting extended family, hosting a party, or doing some home repairs. Prior communication can prevent a conflict and ensure a relaxing break.

Alternately, you might decide to bring a friend home with you for break. This will not be as adventurous for you, but your new friend has likely never seen your city, done any of the tourist activities in your area, or met your family and old friends. Showing someone else where you come from can be as fun as traveling someplace new. Your new friend will surely enjoy your family's home cooking, and will have fun meeting your siblings and pets. Above all, this is a chance to deepen a new friendship and to show your friend more of your life and personality.

## *Spring Break Packages*

Over the years, you may have developed certain ideas and misconceptions about the spring break phenomenon. You may believe spring break is a wild week of constant partying or you may see it as a relaxing time spent sunbathing on a tropical beach. The truth is that spring break is what you make of it. With extensive planning and a big enough budget, you can transform your break into an exotic vacation. Or you can make a spontaneous decision to go home and visit old friends from high school. But if you're looking for a special spring break trip, you must do some research. Late in the fall semester, you will see a lot of advertisements around campus or on the Internet from companies that offer special spring break vacation packages. Many of these are affordable and include hotel accommodations, food vouchers, and even drink deals. However, you must beware of bargains that seem too good to be true—they probably are.

The first decision you must make is what kind of vacation you want for spring break. Beach packages have long been the most popular among undergraduates, but this is not the only option. In recent years, many companies have begun offering ski vacation packages. If you attend a school in a warmer climate, you should seriously consider heading north for break. If your college is located in a colder area, then the beach may be a good option. However, keep in mind that you don't have to try and fit all your goals into one spring break trip. You will have several spring breaks during your college career, and while you won't be able to afford an elaborate trip every year, you can still try different things each time.

QUESTION?

**Can you go on a cruise during spring break?**
Cruises are definitely a good option for a spring break trip. You can choose the duration of your cruise to match your break period and visit lots of interesting port cities. Cruise packages may be more expensive than other spring break trips, but are usually worth the extra cost. Do your research before committing to one cruise line or program.

The next decision to make about your trip is who to take with you. How many people can split one package? Which friends are fun travel partners? Which friends will get everyone in trouble? Everyone involved must have the same goals for the trip. If half of you want to attend lots of parties and eat at nice restaurants, and the other half of you want to conserve money and sit on the beach all day, there are bound to be conflicts on your trip. You're going on a spring break trip to get away from the pressures and hassles of college life and to truly enjoy yourself. Therefore, you need to choose your group carefully.

## Read the Fine Print

There are a lot of companies offering spring break packages. The glossy photos and well-designed flyers will make promises before you even read the first word of their advertisements. In fact, the first few words probably won't mean a whole lot for your spring break experience, but the last paragraph is critical. Before you sign up for any spring break package, read through every bit of fine print. Be sure you understand all the details before you hand over your money.

Most students don't think about budget when planning a spring break trip. This is a mistake. You need to consider the cost of travel, food, taxes, cover charges, event tickets, tips, and souvenirs when planning your budget. In addition to these expenses, you'll need to plan for phone calls, postcards, and a little bit of extra cash for emergencies.

One detail that you need to seriously consider is lodging. What does "hotel accommodations" mean? Will your hotel be something with one bathroom per bedroom, air-conditioning, and a television? Or will you be in bunk beds sharing a single bathroom with everyone else in the building? Will you and your friends share a private room or will you be in a hostel setting sharing the room with strangers? Ask the company to elaborate on the size, style, and location of the rooms. They might even have a photo they could show you.

Another important element is travel. You can assume that getting to and from your spring break vacation location will be your responsibility, but what about after you are there? If your hotel is three miles from the beach, will a shuttle be provided? Will you have to walk through a rough neighborhood to get to the nightlife? Is there at least a shuttle to get you to and from the airport? If such services are not included in your package and you plan to take taxis, be sure to build that into your spring break budget. And if shuttle services or other travel arrangements are vague, you should exercise extra caution. What looks like a fantastic break package could be a miserable week spent in a third-rate hotel miles from a beach or other entertainment.

One of the most overlooked details of spring break packages is food. You are going on this vacation for the fun, the location, and the friends, but you still have to eat. It is unlikely that your package will include all meals, but some include items such as a continental breakfast or some sort of buffet. Find out what is included and what meals you will have to provide for yourself. And remember to build meals into your spring break budget. Also include items that relate to eating and drinking, such as cover charges for nightclubs. These are the seemingly small expenses that can exhaust your budget before the week is half over.

If you are hoping to let loose on break and violate as many rules as possible, be aware that there are cameras everywhere. You never know when your behavior will be caught on film. You also don't want to have problems with police while you are on break. Explaining such things to your parents or college administrators would be unpleasant, to say the least.

You can always contact the company offering a spring break package and ask them questions about the details of the offer. If they are vague or give only indirect answers, you should be suspicious. If there is no phone number to call with questions, you should disregard the company altogether.

Often the best means of knowing if a spring break package is worthwhile is by asking others. If you know other students who have used a company and they were satisfied with their experience, you can feel better about choosing it. These experienced students will be able to offer you tips, share fun anecdotes, and possibly even show you their photos from the trip.

## Alternate Spring Break Experiences

A completely different type of spring break experience, and one that has been gaining popularity on college campuses in recent years, is a break spent working on community service projects. Many times this sort of spring break is set up by an office or organization on campus. The experience can involve staying at the college or within the local community, traveling to a different part of the country, or sometimes traveling out of the country. While you probably won't be staying in hotels, you will be with other college students and your basic needs will be met.

**QUESTION?**

**Where can you find alternate spring break trips?**
Your campus office of community service or religious life will have some information. Student service organizations, such as Alpha Phi Omega, may also sponsor trips. Local chapters of groups, such as Habitat for Humanity, are also likely to have information. If they aren't out in the open, you'll have to show initiative and find these organizations on your own.

An alternate spring break trip can be hard work. Students who attend these experiences often return to campus tired and sore. However, those same students report a tremendous sense of satisfaction and accomplishment. Don't let the thought of some hard work deter you from this type of experience. The work you will do is completely different from your day-to-day life at college and will ultimately leave you feeling refreshed and enthused. After spring break, when you're explaining how you spent your time to friends at college or family at home, the energy in your voice will convey to them that you were part of something special.

Alternate spring break trips may include working with established organizations, such as Habitat for Humanity, or domestic violence shelters. Some trips will involve living and working at a Native American reservation or nature reserve. You may have the chance to tutor children, assist the elderly, or work on construction projects. There are as many possibilities as there are people in need of your services. Only a week of your time could change the lives of dozens, or even hundreds, of people. Even if you don't plan to participate in one of these programs for your first spring break, be sure to consider it in the future.

## *Why Study During Break?*

Why in the world would someone want to study during spring break? If you are going to do schoolwork, then doesn't it just make sense to stay on campus and set up camp in the library? Absolutely not. Spring break is an optimal time to get away from campus and recharge your batteries as you prepare for the last part of the semester. However, a little studying during this week of rest will serve you very well.

The danger of taking study materials with you on break is that they may be damaged or lost. For this reason you should back up your items—make copies of computer disks and photocopies of notes. Leave your original items at school so you will not fall behind if something happens to your materials on break.

Each semester at college will likely be a little more challenging than the one before. This being the case, if you completely detach from your academic mission, even for just a week, it could be that much harder to regain your focus when you return. To avoid losing your concentration, bring a book to read, some notecards to review, or a notebook to study from. On any spring break trip, you will likely have to wait in an airport or endure a long car ride. And even in the sunniest spots, a storm could keep you off the beach for a day or two of your vacation. Having some light studying on hand for these occasions will help keep you from falling behind and will make it easier to jump back into the semester upon your return to campus.

It is also a good idea to bring a notepad or some blank paper on your trip in case inspiration strikes. It may be that in the middle of a flight to paradise you are struck with the perfect outline for your history term paper. If so, you will have the notebook on hand to record your ideas. Even if you don't end up using it for academic purposes, you can at least use the notebook for games of tic-tac-toe during the flight.

## Quick Trips

Many students don't have the budget to take an elaborate break trip, and some simply have no desire for the traditional trips, service opportunities, or visits home. There are still a variety of options for such students, and they don't necessarily involve studying for hours on end. One-, two-, or three-day trips can provide the perfect getaway to those who want to conserve money and still have some fun.

Break periods give students a wonderful opportunity to take quick trips. For example, if you are "stuck" on campus during a break, consider taking day trips to local attractions. If your campus is close to a national park, a historical monument, or a museum, you have a wonderful opportunity to see something new. Get together with other students who have remained on campus for break and go visit these local attractions.

Another option for a quick trip is visiting old or new friends. You might go see a high school friend who is attending another college. Even if your break does not coincide with his, he may still enjoy having a visitor, showing you around his campus, and introducing you to his friends. If he still has to attend classes while you are visiting, use that time to get some of your own studying done. Another option would be to visit the home of one of your college friends. Someone who lives only a few hours from your college may enjoy having you come over for a day or two. You will get to meet her family, see her home, and probably enjoy some homecooked meals.

Quick trips may also include going to see a show or a concert. If your campus is in or near a large city, or if you can get to one in a day's drive, it is worth seeing what shows or other cultural events are taking place in that city during your break period. This could be a chance to see a Broadway play, a singer you really like, or some other event. Even if you have to spend a night in a hotel and pay for gas, this type of trip is cheaper than other break options. And even if you won't have a tan when classes resume, you will have enjoyed several fun experiences.

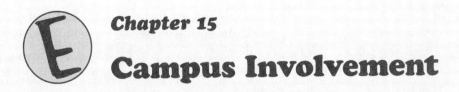

**Chapter 15**

# Campus Involvement

Y ou are going to college for an education but also hope to find a rich life outside of your classrooms. To that end, there are campus organizations available for every student, and joining a few of these groups will improve your social life, strengthen your resume, and help you connect what you are learning in classes to the rest of your life.

# Student Governance

Whether or not you participated in student government during high school, your college will welcome your participation in the formal and informal groups that govern student life on campus. The most obvious group to look for is your student senate. At most schools, the top positions, such as president and treasurer, will be filled in the spring prior to your arrival on campus. However, early in September there will be elections for spots vacated over the summer and perhaps some spaces held for first-year students. Senate seats are usually determined either by class standing, meaning that your entire class must have a certain number of representatives, or by campus geography, meaning that your residence hall must have a certain number of representatives.

Running for a seat in the student senate can be a lot of fun. At most schools you must begin by having a set number of students sign a petition to get you on a ballot. After you achieve this you must start your election campaign. A few schools will have a budget available for candidates, but most of the time you will have to do this on your own. It's a good idea to ask friends to help you think of creative slogans and post flyers around campus.

Membership in the student senate will allow you to:

- Make students' voices heard by administrators and other students
- See how college government really works
- Join committees that fit your interests or career goals
- Develop skills in a real-world environment
- Boost your resume
- Impress your family

Of course, being elected to student senate comes with responsibilities. You must attend the meetings, take information to and from your constituents, and be active in discussions and projects. The more you put into your senate activities, the more rewarding they will be.

There are also other opportunities to participate in student governance. Your residence hall may have a building council that meets weekly to discuss building issues. Often these groups elect voting members, but anybody can attend their meetings. Sometimes they also have budgets to use for social events or equipment purchases, such as a ping-pong table or TV for the lounge. Because these groups meet within your residence hall, they represent a simple opportunity to participate in student governance.

Many colleges have a peer judicial or discipline system. Students who serve as members of these organizations have a wide range of majors and interests; you don't need to be a criminal justice major to join these groups. Peer discipline boards hear cases of alleged violations of college policy. Such cases are often heated and complicated, but the difficult nature of the work makes it that much more rewarding.

Each year, college administrators convene search committees to fill vacant staff positions, and these committees need student representation. Ask your professors or student life professionals, such as hall directors and student activities coordinators, to recommend you when search committees need students. Having a hand in selecting new professors or administrators for your institution is valuable work.

Some residence halls will operate based on a set of community standards. These codes for communal living are less formal than college policies, but are often taken more seriously, and enforced strictly, by members of the community. Similarly, some colleges govern student life according to an honor code. Participating in adjudication boards or standard-setting boards is a powerful way to be involved in student governance.

## *Programming and Activities Boards*

On any given day there are a variety of activities happening across your campus. A handful of these activities are organized and sponsored solely by faculty or staff, but most events occur because students have made them happen. You can become involved in this exciting experience by joining one of the many programming boards on campus.

Your student activities office is probably the hub of event planning on campus. The administrators in this office work with students to help sponsor fun and meaningful activities for the campus community. They will have opportunities for students to join programming boards for big concerts, fall and spring festivals, homecoming events, comedians and other specialized entertainment, and cocurricular events, such as lectures and exhibitions. The student activities office is also likely to have a sizeable budget and needs student help to determine how best to spend that money.

**FACT**

A fringe benefit of serving on an activities committee is the opportunity to meet performers that you bring to campus. The band or comedian you are sponsoring may be just one step from national stardom, and you will have the opportunity to get a photo with them or a signed CD. Your experiences will also make good stories to tell your friends and family.

Simply approaching your student activities office is the easiest way to get involved on a campus programming board. In most cases, you will not have to be elected, but you will need to regularly attend all meetings and help set up and clean up after events. While you can certainly volunteer for a committee that especially interests you, be sure to inquire about committees with only a few members. If you join a small committee, you will have the opportunity to have a larger voice right from the start.

## Religious and Cultural Organizations

Many students come from particular religious backgrounds and hope to join similar worship groups at college. Others have strong ties to their cultural heritage or community and want to continue that affiliation while at college. And some students are simply interested in learning more about different faiths and cultures. Most campuses have a wide variety of organizations suited to meet these needs and interests, and each group will welcome new students as members.

Some religious organizations have formal groups on campus; the Newman Society and Hillel are examples. These groups provide members with a spiritual community where they can engage in discussions, celebrate holidays, and organize activities. Some provide worship opportunities or are affiliated with a local worship center. Many campus religious organizations also try to educate others about religious and cultural issues. For example, Hillel might hold a Passover meal event that is open to the entire college community. Jewish and non-Jewish students can attend and learn about Jewish culture, enjoy cultural dishes, and meet new people. Many religious organizations will also try to cosponsor events with groups, giving members the opportunity to learn about another faith.

Religious organizations offer students the chance to continue practicing a lifelong faith, begin practicing a new religion, or just become a part of a new community. These commitments can be very simple—if you only plan to attend meetings once in a while—or you can take on more responsibility by becoming an event coordinator or the treasurer of the group's funds. If you are interested in learning about the religious organizations offered at your college, ask your activities office staff for information.

Culture and religion are closely intertwined for many students, and religious organizations often help students connect to their cultural heritage while they're away. In other cases the two are slightly or completely different, and for these students, involvement with a cultural organization helps bridge the gap between a home community and a new college life. At most colleges, there are organizations to accommodate almost any cultural group.

Even if you have no religious background, you can still attend services, meetings, and events for most campus religious groups. If you are interested in a particular group, consider attending a meeting or mass with a friend who is already a member. She can give you a little background about the organization, as well as introduce you to her friends in the group.

Though you can certainly seek them out yourself, advertisements for these groups will be posted all over your campus. You are also likely to hear about them by word-of-mouth. They will sponsor cultural exhibitions, meals, dances, and education sessions. Participating in such organizations is a good way to keep in touch with your culture, meet people who share some of your beliefs and values, and teach the rest of the community about your heritage.

## Service Organizations

Many students already have experience with community service before coming to college. For some, it was required as part of the high school curriculum, and others chose to do it for the experience or to spend time with friends working for a valuable cause. These students arrive on campus seeking familiar opportunities. Other students who have never done community service may be interested in trying something new or are looking for a way to make friends. But whether you have prior experience or not, most community service organizations welcome new members year-round.

Some students do service individually, perhaps by teaching children at a local worship center or elementary school. Athletes will often perform service, such as running clinics or organizing park cleanup programs, as part of team membership. But for most students, community service is completed through established organizations. Some community service organizations include:

- Alpha Phi Omega
- Circle K
- Habitat for Humanity
- Rotaract
- Amnesty International
- Big Brothers, Big Sisters

Students who are interested in doing other types of service can work through local agencies. Often your student activities or religious life office will have a list of such agencies. These opportunities often include:

- Literacy programs
- Food banks
- Domestic violence shelters
- Public libraries
- Homeless shelters

While such activities often involve a significant commitment, in terms of time and emotional energy, they are tremendously rewarding for students. If your preferred community service is not represented on your campus, consider organizing a group of students and pursuing resources to help you engage in that service. The service you provide will greatly enrich your college experience, have a positive effect on your community, and leave you with many fond memories.

# Greek Life

Fraternities and sororities are among the most well known social organizations on any college campus. Choosing to join a Greek organization is a big decision and one that you should consider carefully. You will have to separate fact from fiction and let go of your preconceived notions about these groups in order to make the decision that's right for you. Consider the following advantages and disadvantages of Greek membership and speak with friends and family before choosing to join.

## Advantages of Greek Membership

You may have heard quite a few stories about what goes on inside fraternity and sorority houses. You may also have seen movies and TV shows that put a certain spin on these groups. Very often they are portrayed as places where members do nothing but throw wild parties, and some think Greek involvement means you don't have to pay attention to schoolwork. However, these extreme stereotypes are rarely true. Greek organizations have persisted because they are valuable to their hosting colleges and to their members.

**FACT**

Fraternities are regarded as organizations for men and sororities as organizations for women, but many sororities were originally founded as fraternities for women. In casual conversation, it's appropriate to separate fraternities and sororities according to gender, but if you join an organization, take an interest in its history and find out how it was founded.

The most immediate benefit of joining a fraternity or sorority is the camaraderie and friendship that exists in these organizations. These men and women choose to unite based on shared values, goals, and interests. They get to know each other well and learn to depend on each other through good times and bad. While participating in the full breadth of Greek activities, students develop a deep bond with their chosen brothers and sisters, and for many students, this bond lasts a lifetime.

Another benefit of joining a Greek organization is leadership development. As a member, you will have the chance to hold a meaningful office and help direct your organization. You will also benefit from student-to-student mentoring and possibly from alumni mentoring. Your chapter will sponsor speakers or workshops designed to make all members more effective leaders. Greek chapters also tend to encourage their members to vie for leadership roles outside of the chapter. On many campuses, Greek members hold the top leadership positions in student organizations, such as newspaper editor and student government president.

These organizations also perform a remarkable amount of community service each year. Many chapters have a particular cause or agency that they work closely with, and some have several that they work with throughout the course of the year. Such service translates into valuable experience, good citizenship, and important parts of a resume. You get to work side by side with your good friends and make a genuine difference in your local community. You also get the chance to earn positive attention for your chapter and your school. Though good deeds rarely get national news coverage, local news organizations will often highlight a Greek chapter participating in a park cleanup or helping to repaint a local shelter.

One of the greatest benefits of joining a fraternity or sorority, particularly one that is nationally or internationally affiliated, is the opportunity for networking. In addition to your fellow members, each campus chapter will have alumni who are eager to assist you during your college years and beyond. You are also likely to be plugged into a national network of alumni of your fraternity or sorority. You may attend a college in the Midwest and find that you have fraternity brothers or sorority sisters on both the east and west coasts. When you are looking for a job and need to make professional connections, these alumni networks can be invaluable.

Each fraternity and sorority is founded on a specific set of principles. An organization may have a creed or formal statement of values. If the organization treats these principles as more than words on paper and attempts to live up to the values in a meaningful way, students benefit even more from membership in the Greek organization. A written code that is not followed has no value. Each member must abide by the principles of the organization for it to be a complete and successful group.

Other benefits of Greek membership include academic support while you are a student. Some chapters maintain study libraries complete with lecture notes or test guides for specific classes or professors. Many chapters will organize study groups for members taking the same class, and often an older member who has already had that class can serve as a tutor. Some chapters recognize or reward members who do well on assignments, achieve high GPAs, or show the most academic improvement. A few organizations even have scholarship support for members who live up to the ideals of the chapter. And many organizations offer some sort of group housing, often in conjunction with the school, which allows you to live with your closest friends.

Fraternity or sorority networking will certainly benefit you after graduation, but it can also help you while you are in school. Alumni from your organization may be able to help you get a summer job or internship. Your fraternity or sorority may also have local alumni advisors who can act as tutors for classes that are particularly difficult.

## Disadvantages of Greek Membership

Greek membership is not for everyone, and there are very good reasons for an individual to decide against joining a fraternity or sorority. A significant disadvantage of Greek membership, for some, is the necessary time commitment. You will be expected to participate in a wide variety of activities and attend all formal functions. This includes meetings, seminars, and social events. If you are actively involved in other campus organizations or intercollegiate athletics, you may find it hard to manage all of your commitments in addition to your academic responsibilities.

**QUESTION?**

**What is the difference between a local and a national fraternity or sorority?**
Local chapters exist only on your campus and national (or international) organizations exist on many college campuses. National organizations have resources for training, risk management, insurance, and alumni networking. Local chapters tend to be short-term groups though they sometimes petition to join a national fraternity or sorority.

Similarly, Greek life involves a lot of social interaction with the other members of your chapter and of other chapters on campus. If you prefer to be by yourself or with a small group of friends, then joining a Greek organization will present a big challenge for you. Some students also struggle to maintain friendships outside of the fraternity or sorority, particularly on larger campuses. A possible expectation at a fraternity or sorority may be that your brothers or sisters come first. If this is the case, you may have trouble finding time for other friends.

One thing you should consider is that fraternities and sororities require dues. These funds help pay for chapter insurance, membership materials, and other education resources. While the amount varies by chapter, dues can be a significant expenditure for someone on a tight budget. Even if you can manage the dues—either alone or through scholarship help from the chapter—you will be expected to pay for other things during your membership. If chapter members want to sponsor a party with alcohol, they will not be able to use chapter funds; members are informally expected to purchase it on their own. There will also be T-shirts for the chapter and numerous special events, and you will need to buy gifts for your big brother or little sister in the chapter.

One of the biggest disadvantages of membership in a Greek organization is hazing. Though virtually every school and national Greek organization has rules prohibiting hazing, forms of it still take place on most campuses. It is difficult for colleges to catch much of the hazing that occurs, and students who deeply desire membership in a particular organization are often reluctant to say "no" to dangerous or humiliating activities. Hazing does not just mean potential danger for students, but it also may be an indication that the organization does not respect the individual and does not subscribe to its supposed code of values. If you have heard hazing is a part of a particular organization's membership ritual, avoid the group, for your own safety. There are certainly other organizations that will show concern for your well-being.

## Learning Communities

Many colleges are exploring the benefits of learning communities, and each school defines a learning community differently. In general, a learning community strives to move formal learning beyond the classroom. Most learning communities are organized as living-learning areas and involve a residence hall, suite, or house. In addition to living together, you and your colleagues in the community will take a class or series of classes together and/or participate in seminars, lectures, or retreats outside of class time.

It is common that students who share academic interests also have other interests in common, such as preferred extracurricular activities, career aspirations, and music or movies. By participating in a learning community you can engage in an academic interest with other students who are like you in a variety of ways. Not only will you further your education, but you will also build a group of friends with whom you can enjoy discussions and activities. Additionally, you will probably get to know professors beyond the classroom. This can be a lot of fun, and it will help you when you need advice or letters of recommendation as well.

**FACT**

The term "learning community" can be defined very differently from campus to campus. At some schools, they are founded on an academic component. At other schools, a learning community is more of an affinity group, comprised of students who choose to live together due to a shared interest. It is your responsibility to decide if your school's definition fits your goals.

Learning communities do involve a time commitment, and even if you enjoy participating in such a community, you will need to keep a balanced schedule so that your other academic and social commitments don't suffer. Some students find that learning communities are too focused on academics and cocurricular activities and lead to the exclusion of extracurricular activities. If you are not able or willing to devote the necessary time to being a member of a learning community, you may want to avoid this commitment.

## Special Interest Groups

Special interest groups cover a wide range of formal and informal topics. Each academic department usually has an affiliated club advised by a professor or group of professors. Language departments are a good example of this; they often have clubs that sponsor film series, meals, discussions using only the particular language, and even trips to observe cultural events or displays. Sometimes language programs will sponsor a house or residence hall floor where only that language is spoken. These are generally open to both native and non-native speakers.

Departments such as biology and economics will also often have active clubs on campus. These groups exist not only for students who find the topics fascinating—many people who have a casual interest in these areas enjoy the discussions and trips these groups sponsor as well. The biology club is likely to visit a state park to examine plants and animals in the area, as well as enjoy the scenery. An economics club may visit the city's financial center and give members a chance to network with influential business leaders.

Some formal groups exist outside of academic departments. Your campus may have an organization dedicated to environmental sustainability that meets regularly, educates the campus, and works with the administration concerning a number of issues. If such a group has housing on campus the members are likely to model an environmentally friendly lifestyle by choosing to recycle and conserve energy.

Theme floors are popular at many colleges. You can choose from a wide variety of options—anything from an intensive study floor to a specific language-based floor. Such floors give you the opportunity to live with students who have similar values and interests without formally being part of an organization. Additionally, your RA or other students on the floor will probably sponsor programs geared toward the floor's theme.

Similarly, your college may have a group of students who are interested in artistic expression. They may focus on specialty areas, such as singing, painting, and dance, or group themselves as one large organization. These art expression groups tend to be very active on campus and may sponsor shows, take members to events in the local area, and encourage students to express their individuality.

Most campuses have a group for gay, lesbian, bisexual, and transgender students, as well as their friends. These organizations vary greatly; some focus on member support and others on campus activism. Some will be very private groups—not publishing membership lists or holding open meetings. Others will have office space in the student union or housing on campus.

Though there are many formal special interest groups on campus, the informal special interest groups are more numerous and often more important to students. Such a group might consist of the friends you always eat dinner with, or the people you decide to live with in a suite or off-campus apartment. Such affiliations will not feel like special interest groups to you, but that is precisely what they are. You will choose to affiliate yourself with a group of people because of common interests and values. These are the people you are comfortable with, who you can spend a lot of time with, and who are there for you when you need support.

**QUESTION?**

**What if you can't find what you are looking for in existing special interest groups?**

Consider starting a group focused on your particular interest. If you gather a group of students who share your interest, you can lobby your school for the resources necessary to begin a new special interest group. You will also gain valuable leadership experience by enduring the start-up process.

## Finding Your Place

As a new student the variety of social options available to you may seem overwhelming. However, the key is to follow your instincts. Most groups on campus will provide you with fun activities and great friends. But because you won't have time to do everything, you will need to make difficult choices. When you are considering an organization, ask yourself the following questions:

- Do you feel comfortable with other members of the group?
- What time commitment is involved?
- What are the requirements of membership?
- What does the group offer you, other than a fun group to hang out with?
- What financial commitment is expected from you?
- Will membership support your academic or career goals?
- Are there leadership opportunities available for you?
- Do the organization's goals and values match your own?

As you examine each organization and ask these questions, discuss your options and thoughts with friends and family. The people who know you best will sense any reservations you have and be familiar with your goals and values. Sometimes you will disagree with friends and family, but be certain to listen to their feedback. Be sure to pay the most attention to those who have known you the longest. After careful consideration, you can choose the group that's right for you.

Trust yourself and your instincts, even if you cannot articulate your reasons for making a decision regarding a group. If you feel comfortable with the other people who are in the learning community or fraternity, then that might be the right choice for you. If you are happy with an individual approach to life on campus, you may not benefit from joining a group. If all your friends are joining a sorority or club, but something about it doesn't feel right to you, then you shouldn't join. However, if you do make the wrong decision the first time around, don't worry. Every new semester will offer you the chance to re-evaluate your commitments.

There are a variety of social groups on campus that will seek to have you as a member. Most will offer something beyond the social scene, such as leadership development or community service opportunities. Your challenge will lie in choosing which organizations to join, so consider your choices carefully.

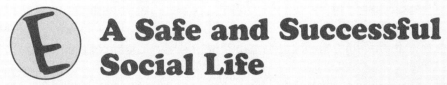

Chapter 16

# A Safe and Successful Social Life

Initially, you will want to do everything you can at college. You will aspire to join almost every club and attend every party, concert, and comedy show available on campus. However, you will quickly discover that even if you gave up classes, studying, and exercise, you still would not have enough time to attend every activity or club meeting. As you learned in Chapter 11, navigating a successful college experience is all about time management. Remember this as you consider other options in the social scene.

# Parties

Parties are an important part of the college experience. A balanced lifestyle includes having fun, as well as studying, working, and exercising. Parties give students a chance to escape the rigors of classes, meet and form friendships with others, and play games, listen to music, or dance. However, with such a wide array of party options available to you on campus, you'll need to choose carefully. You must take several issues into account, including the host, the time, the location, and the mood or theme of the party.

If you plan to visit several parties on a particular night, be sure to travel with a group of reliable friends. Together, make a pact not to leave a party unless every member of the group is accounted for. Having friends with you while you attend parties will not only ensure your safety while walking or driving to your destinations, but it will also mean you have people looking out for you while you are at the party.

Remember that most parties are late-night events. Those that happen on weeknights may keep you from getting to class the next day or completing your studying for that class. Sometimes that will be a risk worth taking, but certainly not on a regular basis. Weekend parties are more numerous and are easier to fit into your schedule. You will also meet a wider range of people at these parties. However, you should not consider weekend party attendance a rule. If you have a term paper that must be finished by the following Monday, you should consider staying in to work on it. The social scene is important and must have a place in your schedule, but always make sure that academics are your first priority.

## School-Sponsored Parties

The largest parties on campus will probably be those sponsored by your college. These will also range from small to large, from general to theme-based, and from one-time to recurring events. Your college's student activities office or student programming board will plan events throughout the school year using money from your activities fee and other sources. In a sense, these activities represent your tax dollars at work, so you are well advised to take advantage of some of them.

Some events will attract everyone—students, faculty, and staff. Most campuses have fall and spring festivals that consist of live music, games, vendors, demonstrations, and other activities. Often the campus food service will have a cookout in conjunction with these activities. These all-day events are a great chance to get out and have fun while meeting a lot of people. You are likely to converse with lots of other students, whether you're waiting in line for food or enjoying the live music.

Your college will also host parties or events scheduled around school traditions. During homecoming week there may be an all-college dance and sometimes the election of a homecoming king and queen. Your school may also have an annual all-college formal dance. These events are particularly enjoyable, giving everybody the chance to dress up and offering students and faculty a chance to get to know each other outside of the classroom. Such events also do a lot to build school spirit.

Many college-sponsored parties will be one-time events organized by the student activities office. A DJ or band will be hired to play for a few hours, usually on a weekend and late at night. These events are generally successful because the school has money to bring good entertainment to campus, and students have some say in what music or theme to have for the party. These events will also be designed to appeal to the diversity on your campus. By attending these school-sponsored parties you can hear anything from country music to hip-hop, and can dance and mingle with a lot of people.

**FACT**

College-sponsored events have the advantage of being free or very cheap for college students. At no other time in your life will you enjoy such a broad range of subsidized entertainment. You have the opportunity to be out with good friends and meet new people, and still maintain your budget. Take advantage of these opportunities whenever they fit into your schedule.

Student organizations will also sponsor parties. These are usually very well attended because students want to support their organization or their friends. It can be great fun to see your new friends show off their culture's music, food, and traditions. Your friend in the Middle-Eastern club may teach you native dances and a little bit about his culture. And many clubs will combine efforts to co-sponsor dances designed to appeal to all students. The African-American club may co-sponsor an event with the Latin-American club, bringing a great deal of diversity and energy to the event.

## Private Parties

Many of the parties sponsored by the school or student organizations will center on dancing, music, or cultural displays. At these events, you'll see a lot of people, have some fun, and learn something new. Because these events are sponsored and monitored by the school they are usually safe and conveniently located. However, for some students these events are too tame or are not attractive because they are officially sanctioned. If this is your opinion, beware: Private parties can be a lot of fun, but they may also present more risks than college-sponsored entertainment.

Before heading to a private party, talk to your friends about expectations for the evening. Make sure that you are all watching out for each other and that you all leave the party together. Walking home is more fun if you are with good friends, and you will also be much safer if you are in a large group.

Most private parties will happen off campus. These will almost always be in houses or apartments of upperclassmen and will usually feature alcohol. The hosts will likely charge guests a few dollars at the door in order to pay for the alcohol. Rarely will these parties sell individual drinks because the hosts believe that they can't get in trouble if they don't actually sell alcohol to minors. This is not the case. The truth is that any party where alcohol is served may draw the attention of local law enforcement, and if you are caught drinking alcohol illegally, you could be penalized. While a small gathering of close friends who can legally drink alcohol is probably safe, attending a large party featuring alcohol where you do not know the hosts can put your health and legal reputation at risk. Carefully consider a party's host, location, and theme before you attend.

There will also be private parties held in residence halls hosted by people on your floor or students on other floors of your hall. Before attending such a party, keep in mind that more than four or five people can crowd a residence hall room and make for an uncomfortable gathering. Someone else in the building is bound to complain to an RA or security staff member if such a party grows too large or causes too much noise. It is best to avoid these gatherings and thus avoid an almost certain encounter with the college discipline system. However, if you would simply like to hang out in your room with a few friends to watch a movie, you will probably be safe and comfortable.

## Personal Safety

At college your safety and well-being will be primarily your responsibility. This is a change that you need to adapt to quickly. Much of what you need to know about personal safety seems like common sense, such as locking your residence hall room door when you are out or when you are sleeping. However, each year many college students are lulled into a false sense of security. While college is a generally safe place, students who let down their guard for too long often end up victims of theft or other crimes. Exercising caution in all situations will help you ensure your safety.

In addition to keeping your room locked, you should also keep cash and valuables hidden in drawers or secured in a small safe or lockbox. Items that are left in the open are easily seen and make prime targets for thieves. Even textbooks are sometimes stolen; they can be sold to other students or returned to the campus bookstore. You will likely feel safe in your residence hall because RAs and security staff do regular rounds and there is a locked or monitored front door for your building. However, you are partly responsible for the safety of your residence hall. Never prop exterior doors, never let someone into the building if you don't know him, and always report suspicious activity or safety hazards to your RA as soon as possible. These simple things will significantly contribute to the safety of everyone who lives in your residence hall.

When you are walking around campus, it's a good idea to walk with a few friends. As you are walking, be aware of your surroundings and the people nearby. Stay in well-lit areas and know where you're going before you leave your room. Always make sure that a roommate or friend knows where you're going and when you expect to return. Don't carry a lot of cash and only take credit cards with you if you know you'll need them.

**QUESTION?**

**Should you have pepper spray or mace with you at college?**
While these items seem like a good idea they can easily go wrong. The spray may not disable your attacker or may not function correctly. And an experienced attacker can easily turn the spray against you. Some colleges have policies against having such sprays on campus, so check with your security office before purchasing these products.

If you have to travel across campus alone after dark, call ahead and tell someone that you are on your way. Also, check with your security office to see if an escort is available. Many colleges will hire students or other staff to work at escorts for students. These staff members or professional security officers can walk with you across campus and report any suspicious activity they see on the way. The escort will probably be wearing a uniform, but if not, ask for an ID if you are at all suspicious of the person. Sometimes an escort service will give you a ride to your destination, and in cold or rainy weather a dry, warm car is a much better alternative to walking.

Most colleges will offer self-defense classes, either for academic credit or as special seminars. Such classes are a good opportunity to learn some new skills and meet other people. However, learning self-defense does not make you safer. Self-defense is only useful once you have been attacked, and your goal is to keep from being attacked in the first place. You should take advantage of such classes, but don't mistake your new skills for invulnerability. As a rule, always be alert and aware of your surroundings, avoid risky situations, and trust your instincts.

Traditional martial arts programs don't teach skills that are designed for self-defense situations. While such programs have great athletic and artistic value, if you are specifically interested in learning self-defense tactics, choose a program that teaches in a simple and direct manner. Your campus safety office will know what is offered on campus or in the local community.

## Finding Love

Many students come to college looking for a good education, great friends, an active social life, and sometimes love. But where does one go on a college campus to find love? Opportunities are everywhere, but if you look too hard you will miss most or all of your chances. Keep in mind that you have a lot of time to find love. Focus on your studies and on meeting a lot of people; from there you will naturally find people you really like, people you want to spend more time with, and people you love.

That being said, most students do find a balance between academic responsibility and a romantic life. There are many places to meet people, but most students start looking at parties on campus. A party may be a good place to meet someone, but due to the loud music or crowded atmosphere, it is probably not a good time to get to know a person well. However, a party is a good place to see what people are like in public, identify those who are outgoing and like to have fun, and perhaps get to know classmates on a more social level.

Classes and study groups are surprisingly good places to find love. You'll find other students who have something in common with you and who you'll see regularly, at least for the semester. Studying with a person gives you insight into his academic goals, his personality, and his outlook on life. And even if you don't find love in a study group or classroom, you may still meet a great friend or study partner.

One of the best ways to meet interesting people is through your friends. Your roommate or a friend who lives in another residence hall may introduce you to someone, or a friend may invite you to join a new group of people for lunch or dinner. People who know you well often make good recommendations; they know what you like, what you dislike, and what you are like as a friend.

If you regularly attend campus events, you may see the same people again and again. This probably alludes to common interests and the potential for a good friendship. If you see the same guy every time you attend a basketball game, for example, perhaps you should consider introducing yourself to him. If you get along well, you will have a new friend who will in turn introduce you to other people. Even if you don't end up dating this person, you will at least have someone to sit with at basketball games in the future.

When looking for love, you are simultaneously searching for someone and trying to attract someone. Part of your attractiveness is your physical appearance, but a bigger component is your attitude. Be positive and friendly when meeting new people. Laugh with others instead of at them. And having a breath mint handy can't hurt either.

Many people find that an intense search for love is rarely successful. It's more likely that you will meet a special person in very casual or unexpected circumstances. This could be the person who always does laundry at the same time as you, or another student who attends the local worship center that you prefer. Love generally turns up where you least expect to find it. So, relax, enjoy the company of others, and treasure a special relationship when it comes along.

Finding love requires a lot more than going to the right places and meeting the right people. Unfortunately, many people you meet will be looking for something very different than you are. Some people are only looking for sexual partners, some are only looking for friends, some have a boyfriend or girlfriend at home or at another college, and very few are looking for true love. Moreover, you cannot tell what each person is looking for and there is no easy way to ask, at least initially. So, to protect your health and your feelings, be sure to identify what you're looking for before you head out in search of love.

**What if you are in love with someone from home?**
It can be hard to make a long-distance relationship work, but students do this successfully all the time. Trust and honesty are two traits these couples must possess, and they must work to have open and frequent communication in order to make the relationship work from far away.

People who want something can be dishonest and manipulative, either intentionally or unintentionally. A person who only wants a sexual partner may say anything to sway your decisions. People who desperately want to fall in love may deceive themselves about what they like or who they really are. The longer you know someone, the better sense you have of who that person really is. Typically, this means seeing one person exclusively.

## Dating

Dating has been referred to as a lost art on college campuses. More often students tend to attend parties in groups, have brief relations with one another, and then move on. Couples tend to be those students who have known each other for a long time without ever having really dated. While it is less common, one-on-one dating certainly does occur on college campuses. If you're unsure of the type of person you are looking for, dating people casually might be a good option.

Fortunately, your college campus is full of fun and easy dating opportunities. When you have found one person who you want to get to know better consider these activities:

- See a movie on campus or at a local theater
- Go to a sporting event
- Watch TV in your room or the residence hall lounge
- Eat dinner off campus
- Take a walk through a residential neighborhood

- Go to an amusement park
- Visit a local tourist attraction
- Study together
- Go to a campus dance
- Go to a local nightclub
- Visit an art show or campus museum

While you're dating, there are two important things to keep in mind. First, be a good listener. This will impress the person you're dating and will allow you to get to know her better. You should listen to her whole statement before trying to think of a response, and don't interrupt her when she is telling a story. Second, and perhaps the most important, be yourself. You want to know who she really is and she wants to know the same things about you. If you try to uphold a false identity, dating will be more difficult. Telling lies or exaggerating stories will only mislead and confuse your date.

If you are interested in dating someone, ask! If the person says "no," then you are no worse off than before. Many people have misconceptions about who is supposed to ask for a date, in terms of gender. These days, most of these ideas aren't regarded as rules. So, whether you're a man or a woman, if you're interested in someone, make your feelings known.

Successful dating does not mean that you and he will be together forever. Dating is a process through which you get to know someone better, and you will likely date many people before you find one special person who you want to be with for a long time. It is rare that a person marries the first person he dates. To fully appreciate this, ask your parents and relatives how many people they dated before finding their spouses. Their answers may surprise you. If you go on a few dates and things aren't clicking, don't think of the dates as failures. Every time you date someone you always learn a little more about yourself.

Another hallmark of successful dating is that neither person is hurt or taken advantage of during the dating process. When you first start dating someone new, you may not know what his true intentions are. This being the case, you will have to take certain measures to protect yourself. Here are some tips for your dating safety:

- Never go someplace unfamiliar with someone you don't know well
- Meet at the date location instead of riding in an unfamiliar person's car
- Tell a friend where you are going, with whom, and when you will be back
- Carry a cell phone and a small amount of extra cash
- Never do something that makes you feel uncomfortable
- Stay in public places with someone you don't know well
- Don't drink alcohol until you know your date well

Emotional hurt is much harder to guard against while dating. Sometimes a match only disappoints one person, and the other is left confused and hurt. If you're the person who wants to stop dating, the best thing to do is be honest with the other person. This may be difficult, but it is the right thing to do. If you're the person who is emotionally hurt then give yourself time to feel sad but don't wallow in your sadness. Try to get out and do things with your friends again soon after the relationship ends. Remind yourself that there is a vast world outside your door, and that you will have thousands of opportunities to date others in the future.

## Sex

By this point in your life, you have probably received lectures about sex on several occasions. You're not confused about where babies come from, you're probably aware of the many reasons to use contraception, and you're familiar with family and religious views on premarital sex. At the same time, you have seen an increasing amount of sex on television, in the movies, and even in video games. Advertisers know that sex sells products, particularly to the college-age market. How you approach sex while at college will be one of the most important decisions of your college career and perhaps your life.

The absolute safest choice you can make is to abstain from sex. This will protect you from an unwanted pregnancy, sexually transmitted diseases, and other emotional or physical harm. Students who choose abstinence report that they have just as much fun as everyone else at college, have fewer emotional crises, and are still accepted by their friends. Abstinence is a choice, and one that you should consider seriously.

You and your new friends will certainly talk about sex, no matter what your intentions are. In the process, you will identify friends who have similar thoughts or values. Talking to these people regularly and openly about sex can help you maintain your resolve to stick to your values, and you will likewise help your friends stick to theirs.

If you choose to have sex while at college, you need to protect yourself physically and emotionally. You should start by deciding what circumstances will lead you to having sex. How long do you need to know your partner, and what do you need to know about him, before you have any form of sexual contact? Also, what type of sexual contact are you willing to engage in? Know your limits before you get involved in a sexual encounter. If you don't want to do something, be certain to express that clearly early in the encounter.

If you decide to have sex, use some form of protection. You want to avoid getting a sexually transmitted disease, as well as pregnancy. Latex condoms are the most popular and widely recommended safe-sex device. However, even condoms can't provide 100 percent protection from diseases or guard completely against pregnancy. For this reason, it's wise to use two forms of contraception when engaging in sexual acts.

There are a variety of birth control methods available over the counter. The type of birth control you want to use is a very personal decision. Talk to your health center staff or primary physician about birth control. Your conversation will be confidential and you can learn about what is available, the risks involved with each method, and other important facts. Your health and safety must be your primary concern, and it will be largely your responsibility.

Safe sex is the responsibility of both partners. If you are unable to have an open conversation about this, you and your partner need to wait before having sexual contact. If you talk about this issue early on in your relationship, you'll be prepared for planned or spontaneous sexual encounters.

## Alcohol and Other Drugs

For many years, alcohol and other drugs have been prevalant on college campuses. Generations of students recall good times involving alcohol and drugs, but others learned about the dangers of these substances the hard way. Whether or not to drink alcohol or take drugs is a highly important and personal decision that you will likely be forced to make while at college. But before you choose to do anything, educate yourself about the risks involved in taking drugs.

### Alcohol

Alcohol is the drug of choice on most college campuses, and it remains one of the most difficult issues colleges must face. Many college students feel that drinking alcohol is a right of passage and that related laws are unjust or unnecessary. However, alcohol is connected to more student problems than any other single factor. Students who consume alcohol irresponsibly often find themselves in dangerous situations or in trouble with law enforcement, get lower grades in classes, and experience poor interpersonal relationships with peers and family.

Some students drink alcohol responsibly and successfully at college, rarely experiencing any of the negative consequences. These students typically drink smaller quantities and less frequently than their peers. They also never drink on an empty stomach and know how much they can drink before getting sick or even intoxicated. These students tend to be more successful on all fronts. Unfortunately, other college students don't drink responsibly. The goal among many students is to become intoxicated as quickly as possible. While in this state, these students feel that they are funnier, stronger, and more popular than when they are sober. In truth, they usually seem ridiculous or prove dangerous to the other students at a party.

A frightening danger of alcohol use is the amount of time it takes the body to process alcohol. In general, one beer, a glass of wine, and a one-ounce shot of liquor each contain the same amount of alcohol. It will take your body approximately one hour to process one ounce of alcohol. So, it is a good idea to limit yourself to one drink per hour, as long as you don't drink for hours on end. However, it's important to keep in mind that different drinks are usually consumed at different paces. While a beer is sipped over time, a shot is usually consumed all at once. Four shots in one hour will be more difficult for your body to manage than four beers in four hours.

You and your roommate should discuss alcohol and drugs thoroughly. If one roommate is constantly sneaking alcohol into the room, the other is made just as vulnerable to punishment. And if one roommate is constantly coming home drunk and making a mess in the room, the other suffers. Be sure to speak honestly with your roommate about these issues as soon as possible.

Your weight and body fat also affect how your body processes alcohol. Heavier people can usually drink more without feeling the effects of alcohol. However, a person with low body fat will feel the effects of alcohol more quickly than a person of similar body type who has more body fat. For example, a 200-pound linebacker will feel the effects of alcohol sooner than a 200-pound couch potato.

Students who are new to drinking are at a greater risk in social situations. Peer pressure can lead these students to drink too much and too quickly, resulting in getting sick or becoming dangerously incapacitated. Also, men, who tend to be larger and thus able to consume more alcohol, may pressure women to keep up drink-for-drink and then take advantage of them. Alcohol is the most widely used drug among sexual predators. To protect yourself, always keep track of how much you're drinking, have a close friend keep an eye on you during a party, and if you feel sick or uncomfortable, stop drinking immediately.

Mixed drinks can be particularly dangerous. Carbonated beverages can get alcohol into your system more quickly. And drinks that contain several kinds of liquor are particularly potent. A mixed drink with three shots will take about three hours to be processed by your body. Use extra caution when drinking cocktails and other mixed drinks at parties.

## Other Drugs

There are many other drugs available on or around most college campuses. Marijuana has been a popular drug among college students for decades. It clearly affects memory and college students in particular can't risk this damage while taking classes. Also, marijuana is easily detectable, so students who use it run a great risk of being caught by college authorities or law enforcement officials.

Ecstasy is another drug that is used in many clubs and on college campuses as well. Repeated used of ecstasy has been shown to do irreparable damage to the human brain. Cocaine, heroin, and LSD are also found on many college campuses. The dangers of these drugs don't only consist of physical effects, but taking drugs can also cause you to suffer academically, socially, and economically. These substances are not only dangerous, but they are also very expensive.

Steroids remain a popular drug choice among a small group of college students. Athletes or students who enjoy working out a lot often take steroids to help their performance. However, steroids can do serious and sometimes irreparable damage to the body, and athletes who are caught using steroids can be excluded from competition, may lose scholarships, and can hurt their team's reputation.

Students with a drug habit can seek confidential help from the counseling center on campus, and those who want to know more about drugs and their effects can speak with the counseling center, health center, or security office. Your RA may also know of other resources. The important thing to remember is that you can always seek help for a drug problem. College officials are more concerned with your well-being than getting you in trouble. The earlier you identify and fix a problem with drugs, the more time you'll have to recover and resume your life.

Drug use can hurt your ability to continue your education or pursue your desired career. Even if you are only caught in possession of drugs once, this offense may come up on a background check when you are applying for jobs four years later. A conviction can also cost you eligibility for scholarships, work-study employment, or study abroad opportunities.

Rohypnol and GHB are two insidious drugs that are very popular among sexual predators, and they are indicative of the hidden dangers that exist in college social scenes. Rohypnol and GHB are typically placed in a drink where they are dissolved and are difficult to detect. The person who consumes these drugs may appear to be okay; however, she is somewhat sedated and may be more open to suggestion. These drugs also create a memory gap for victims. Victims may wake up in a strange place and not remember what happened in the previous few hours. Ketamine, an anesthetic used mostly by veterinarians, and gamma butyrolactone (GBL), an industrial solvent, are also used by predators to disorient and disable their targets. While you should not let this information frighten you to the point of never leaving your room, knowing about these drugs and their effects will help keep you safe.

These drugs are often found at parties where people don't know each other well. Sexual predators don't want to get to know their victims, they only want to have sex or have control over another person. So, when you're at a party and don't know some of the people there, be extra vigilant. Never accept a drink from someone you don't know or only know casually. Never leave your drink unattended, or if you must, abandon that drink and get a new one. Talk to your friends before going to a party and let them know your intentions for the evening. And make a pact to leave as a group no matter what.

**Chapter 17**

# The Art and Science of Studying

College will be a completely different experience than high school, both in and out of the classroom. In addition to social changes, you will find that classes are more difficult and move more quickly, that professors expect more from students, and that your old study habits won't be adequate if you want to earn good grades. At the same time, you are more mature, more flexible, and more goal-oriented than you were in high school, so with a little preparation these challenges will all be manageable.

# *Preparation from Day One*

The successful completion of a class begins with the day you add the course to your schedule. You need to think about how to be successful in that class. This means building the class and study time into your schedule and figuring out what resources are available to you. Find out which of your friends have taken this class or had this professor before, who you know that is majoring in that field, and what kinds of tutoring are available on the topic. Knowing all of this ahead of time will help you get through difficult times quickly.

Of course, you need to pay attention to the basic details as well. Make sure that you purchase the books required for the class. Your campus bookstore will have used and new copies of all the books you will need to complete your coursework. Used copies are cheaper and, if they are not heavily marked, are often just as good as new copies. Some online booksellers will have your textbooks too, but when figuring out the cost of the text, be certain to factor in shipping and handling. Sometimes what looks like a cheaper book is actually just as expensive as the one you can purchase at your bookstore. And be prepared to pay a significant amount for college textbooks; no matter what the subject, they don't come cheap.

**QUESTION?**

**Are tape recorders or laptop computers good things to have for class?** Though these products may help some students in certain cases, the majority of students still stick with the traditional pen-and-paper method. If you find that your handwritten notes are too messy, you may choose to transfer them into your computer in your free time.

You also need to have the standard school supplies: pens, pencils, and notebooks, and sometimes rulers, calculators, or other equipment. Some college students prefer legal pads for taking notes in class. If you go this route choose the kind that is three-hole punched so that you can transfer your notes to a binder. Binders remain the best way to keep your notes organized. In addition to these basic items, you may also need special equipment for a class, such as goggles for a science lab. Make sure that you have everything you need for the class ahead of time.

When you are new to a campus, make sure that you find out where all of your classes will be located ahead of time. Do a practice run of your daily schedule, walking from your residence hall to each of your class locations. This will help you be on time on the first day of class. Before long, finding your way to each classroom will be second nature, but in the beginning it is helpful to have a map of your campus and a copy of your detailed schedule with you at all times.

During your first class meeting, your professor will hand out a syllabus. This is one of the most important documents you will use in the course. This document will spell out expectations, grading procedures, assignment deadlines, and test dates. Transfer important dates to your time-management schedule, keep the syllabus in a safe place, and refer to it often.

If you should happen to lose your copy of the syllabus for a particular class, either ask to photocopy a friend's syllabus, or see if you can download one from the Internet. Many professors post the syllabi for their classes on the college Web site or server. Replacing your lost syllabus yourself is a much better option than bothering your professor for another copy.

## *Attendance and Seating*

Whether or not attendance is a requirement for your class, it is best to attend every day. Some college professors have attendance policies, but many don't. Even those professors who don't keep track of attendance may still grade you on class participation, and you can't participate if you are absent. Whether you attend or not, you are responsible for the material covered in class. You and your family are paying for the class, so missing it is kind of like buying a movie ticket and throwing it away.

In general, class attendance may seem pretty mundane. You will go to class, take notes, study, and return to class. But you never know when something especially interesting or useful will come up in a lecture, discussion, or in-class film. When you miss a class, you may be missing some information that will appear on an upcoming quiz or exam. The more you attend, the better prepared you will be.

If you take a science course with a laboratory component, be especially certain to attend every session. It takes the professor a lot of time to set up each lab, and sometimes there are limited resources for each experiment. This being the case, labs are often one-shot deals and there may be no way to make up missed sessions.

You should try to arrive to your classroom five or ten minutes before the class begins. This allows you to get a good seat and briefly review your notes from the last class meeting. Reviewing your notes in this way primes your brain to receive new information on that topic. And whenever possible, you should try to sit in the first three or four rows of the class. This will ensure that you can see and hear everything that happens in class and will reduce the number of distractions you have to contend with. Some students prefer to sit near the middle of a row to get the best view of everything, but in lecture halls students with long legs often prefer aisle seats so that they can stretch out their legs.

If you miss a class, it is your responsibility to learn the material that was covered. You can always go to the professor and ask what material was discussed and if there were any handouts that you missed. Be certain to check your syllabus so that you have an idea of what was going to be covered that day. After an absence, you should also talk to other students in the class to find out what you missed. Ask to copy another student's notes from that day, but choose to ask only the students you know to be attentive and engaged. However, don't get in the habit of missing class and using others' notes. Your classmates will not appreciate this behavior.

**ALERT!**

If you know that you are going to miss a class, speak to your professor ahead of time. This will let your professor know that you are interested in the material and are not showing disrespect by your absence. And after absences, never ask your professor: "Did we cover anything important in class?" You should consider all of your classes equally important.

# Lectures and Note-Taking

Much of your time in class will be spent listening to lectures and taking notes. If you do this poorly, your preparations for tests will be difficult and often ineffective. Fortunately, note-taking skills can be easily developed over time and with a little bit of concentration. To begin, your notes must include a few basic components, such as the date and overall topic of the lecture. This will help you keep information organized when you need to review later. Also, when you're working with study groups or attending review sessions, you can quickly reference a particular day's lecture notes. If your professor titles his lectures, make a note of that as well.

**ALERT!**

It is important to minimize distractions during class. Don't sit near people who whisper throughout class, always remember to turn off your cell phone, and try not to sit near windows or doors. If there is a clock in the room, make a point to look away from it so that you can focus on the lecture instead of the time.

Another major thing to keep in mind is that lectures usually have a definite structure, just like the papers you write. There will be an introduction, several main points and illustrations, and a brief summary. When your professor begins her lecture, you want to listen carefully for the structure. Try to identify and write down the focus of the lecture. Listen for key words such as "first" or "for example" that indicate important points or transitions. Another thing to do is watch and listen for nonverbal clues about what is important. Your professor's hand gestures, facial expressions, and pauses will add to the material that you are receiving. Some of these clues will help you take notes, indicating which points are more significant than others. Other clues may indicate items that will be on a quiz, related to a paper assignment, or represented on the final exam.

As you are listening to the lecture or discussion for the day, try to connect what is being said with what you have read outside of class or information that has been covered in previous class meetings. This will help you learn the material, understand what is currently being said, and be prepared for class discussions. It's important to participate in class discussions. This gives you an opportunity to check your understanding of the material with the professor, may help your grade, and lets the professor know that you are an enthusiastic and engaged student.

When taking notes, you may choose to leave the right quarter of the page as a margin, perhaps marking it off as a column. While you are writing your class notes use this margin to make side comments. Examples of things to write in this margin are:

- Questions about the material being covered
- Indications that the information will be covered on a test
- References to textbooks or other sources
- Concepts you want to revisit for a paper or essay

If you write questions in the margin, it's important to answer them quickly. Do this in your next study session for the class or approach the professor when the class ends. By the time you get to your next class meeting, all questions should be answered.

If you find that your mind is wandering during a lecture, force yourself to focus on notes from a previous class meeting. This will help you stay focused on the class, will enable you to hear key words that come up in the lecture, and will help you form a good response if the professor unexpectedly calls on you with a question.

As you are taking notes, don't try to write down everything that the professor says. Some information, such as greetings or chatty news is pointless for your notes. Write down only those points and examples that relate to the topic of the lecture. Also, restate what is being said in your own words. This will help you learn the information more quickly and recall it more accurately later. Additionally, try to take notes in outline or bullet form, relying on single-line entries. Paragraphs will be harder to skim through later when you are looking for a particular piece of information. You can also use abbreviations to increase your note-taking speed. If you use an abbreviation that is specific to that class, note its definition in the margin so that you don't confuse yourself later.

## Effective Reading

Though you will have done a lot of reading in high school, you will have to hone your reading skills yet again in college—you will also be expected to read a lot more material in a much shorter amount of time. Moreover, the information you read will reappear on tests, in class discussions, and in the papers you write. In some cases, you will read books or articles that are never addressed by your professor in class; however, you will still have to understand the key concepts in those readings should they come up on an exam.

Reading in bed will only help you do one thing: fall asleep. In order to retain as much material as possible, you should be sitting upright, preferably at a desk, in a well-lit room. If you are reclining in a dim area, you will likely end up using your book as a pillow.

The first key to reading at the college level is to initially read the material completely without taking notes or making marks in your book. You need to get a good sense of all the material that is present before evaluating what is or is not important. Remember that this reading may be more complex than what you're used to, so give yourself plenty of time to complete it.

As you are reading, keep several questions in mind. Your professor has a reason for requiring this reading, and if you can identify this reason you will get more out of the reading. This kind of intentional reading will help you learn things more quickly. Examples of questions to keep in mind are:

- What does your professor hope you will gain by reading this material?
- How does the reading relate to what you are covering in class?

- Can you use the information from the reading for an upcoming paper assignment?
- How is this information similar to or different from other things you are reading in this course?
- How does this information relate to things you are reading in other courses?

After your initial reading, stop and think about how what you just read relates to what your professor has lectured about in class. Then go back through the material and highlight or underline key points. Highlighting too much is not helpful, so be very selective when doing this. In general, if you highlight more than 20 percent of the reading, the technique loses its impact. Consider using a few different highlighters to identify different types of key information. For example, you might choose to use yellow for quotations, blue for key concepts, and green for vocabulary. This will allow you to quickly skim the reading later on and identify important aspects of the section. You may also choose to highlight your notes in a similar manner.

Taking notes on your reading is also a worthwhile exercise. You can start by making notes in the margins of your book. Write down quick questions, points that connect to lectures, or a few words about how you can use the information. Also, take notes as you read through the material a second or third time. You can then use these notes to create index cards for writing papers or studying for exams. Summarizing the material that you are reading in your own words will help you internalize it for later use on tests and in class discussions.

## Study Groups

Studying with a group of friends is not always an effective method of learning material for an exam. While with friends, you may be more tempted to tell jokes than focus on your studies. However, if you exercise discipline, working closely with a small group of others can greatly advance your understanding of a topic and enhance your performance in a class. It's up to you to control experiences when working in groups.

**What if you can't find a group to study with?**
Ask students just before or after class if they are interested in a study group. You can also ask your professor to make an announcement that students interested in joining a group should speak with you right after class. If you're still having trouble, ask your RA or academic advisor for guidance.

The first thing you should do is maintain a small group. One to three other students will give you a variety of perspectives, and with only a few members, everyone will have a chance to speak. You also want to choose these students carefully. For effective studying, you want to work with students who will take the group seriously, who are generally prepared for class, and who have good class attendance. It's okay if the conversation occasionally strays from the task at hand, but the study topic should be the entire group's priority.

At some point, another student will probably ask to borrow your notes. Be cautious about this. Will he return your notes, and if so, will they be in good condition? Never give out all of your notes at once, if at all. Suggest that he copy your notes while you are together, so that nothing happens to your originals. And if you do this favor for someone, feel free to ask the same favor of him when you need help later on.

When your group meets, you should always have a specific purpose in mind. You may want to review the last few lectures, discuss the readings, or figure out how certain concepts are related to the focus of the class. If you come together without having established a purpose, you'll spend a lot of time trying to figure out where to start. The purpose can change as the meeting proceeds, but it at least gives you a starting point for your conversation.

As you're discussing items with the other students, don't allow minor points to distract you. The focus should not fall on the person who participates the most in class, or the one who received the highest grade on the last exam, but rather the group should work as a team to make sure everyone learns the material thoroughly. To this end, everyone must participate in the group's discussions. If two members of the group are actively exploring a topic and the third member is simply writing down everything that's said, then the third person is benefiting from the others' work without making a contribution himself. Group members will likely become upset if each person doesn't do his part.

As far as where to study, choose a location that is comfortable and accessible to everyone in the group. However, be sure that your location isn't too comfortable. If you choose to study on your bed, you may get drowsy and lose your concentration. Your residence hall lounge may be a better place to work. Everyone can gather around a table or grab a spot on the floor, spread out notes, and have a robust discussion. The library is also a good place to go, but you may not be able to have a loud discussion there. Try to find a place where you can bring a lot of materials, where you can speak loudly and candidly, and where you can remain for several hours, if needed.

## Flashcards, Mnemonics, and Other Tricks

There are a variety of little things you can do to learn the material you are studying. One longtime favorite has been the use of mnemonics and acronyms to help students remember things. For example, students who took music lessons as children may remember trying to memorize the lines on the treble staff in music. Many children were taught, "Every Good Boy Deserves a Favor" to remember that the lines are E, G, B, D, and F. You can create similar mnemonics and acronyms for the material you are studying.

Flashcards are also a favorite tool for college students. You can use them for vocabulary words, key names and dates, and focus concepts. You may choose to put the highlighted items in your notes onto flashcards for easy reviewing as well. This will allow you to reorganize your notes into different groups and see how various pieces of information are interrelated.

Visualization is a powerful memory tool for some students. If you can visualize the concept you are working with, you will have at least two ways to recall the information when you need it. Recalling the shape of a continent may help you locate and identify its countries. Similarly, picturing the periodic table of elements, or sketching it on a piece of scrap paper, may help you remember its contents and their details.

An easy and yet often neglected leaning tool is recitation. Going over information several times increases the likelihood that you will recall it when you need to. When you're reading a chapter, stop frequently and recite what you think you've just read. Then go back and read it again to see if your understanding was correct. This works with textbooks, articles, and even class notes. By making your studying an active process, you have a better chance to learn the material.

**ALERT!**

Though there are many tricks that will help you remember key information for an exam, none of these strategies are substitutes for hard work. Multiple-choice test questions appear less frequently in college, so you may need to learn information more thoroughly than you're used to. Plan on studying hard, and only use the tricks to recall information when necessary.

A final trick for superior learning is rest. Your body and your mind need regular rest if they are to function well. There will be times during your college years when it is impossible to get a good night's sleep—you can count on at least one fire alarm at 3:00 A.M. But for the most part, you should be able to get enough sleep to allow your brain to function at the high level necessary in college courses.

## Talking to Professors

Many new students are intimidated by college professors. These people are perceived to be the keepers of knowledge, experts in their fields, and beyond questioning. In truth, college professors are an undergraduate's best allies. They have gone through many years of college and thus know what you are experiencing. They are excited when students are genuinely interested in learning, are often interested in questions and an exchange of ideas, and have lives outside of the classroom.

It makes a lot of sense to talk to your professor about the class you're taking with her. Approaching her with questions about lectures, readings, or the general topic area will help you learn the material better and will let her know that you are genuinely interested. Your professor wants to help you learn, but she won't do the work for you. Sometimes your only choice will be to figure something out for yourself. When you do, go back to the professor and tell her what you discovered. This will give you the opportunity to check your information and will demonstrate your commitment to learning.

It is also acceptable to approach your professor with questions unrelated to course material. Perhaps you are considering a career or major in her field, and she can offer tips on how to pursue your goals. If your professor has children she may need a babysitter; this will offer you the chance to earn income and know your professor better. She may also be known for other interests, such as competing in triathlons or working with a community agency. If you share those interests approach her and ask how to become involved. You can simultaneously engage in an exciting activity and form a stronger relationship with your professor.

**QUESTION?**

### Where and when can you find your professors?
Other than after class and during office hours, you may also see your professors in the library, at a campus coffee shop, at athletic games, or at other events on campus. Don't hesitate to approach your professor in informal settings and have a quick conversation. They're there because they enjoy interacting with students.

Your academic advisor will likely also be a professor, and you should pay special attention to the advice this person gives. The conversations the two of you have about course selections, career plans, graduate schools, personal interests, letters of recommendation, and personal difficulties can be among the most helpful you will have while at college. Also, keep in mind that if your advisor is not helpful or is unresponsive to your questions and concerns, you probably have the option to switch to another advisor. Speak with the head of your academic department if you want to do this.

# Taking Tests

The college experience is a great one. Your basic needs are taken care of, you're in charge of your daily schedule, you're surrounded by people with similar interests and lifestyles, and you probably even enjoy some of the academics. But one element remains constant and continuously causes problems for students: tests. You'll encounter every sort of test at college, and doing a few little things will allow you to perform well without sacrificing your social life.

Remember to get a good night's sleep prior to your test. Double-check that your alarm is set so that you wake up in time to eat a good breakfast on the day of the test. Remember that taking good care of your body will help your brain work better. You want to give yourself every advantage to do well.

It will help if you know what kind of test you will be taking. If it is going to be a short-answer test, you need to be able to explain concepts briefly. If it is a multiple choice or fill-in-the-blanks test, you need to know names, dates, and vocabulary. Usually, the professor will tell you the format of the test ahead of time, but if not, feel free to ask for this information. Even if the professor denies your request, she may offer some other helpful hints or study tips.

You should also have an idea of what the professor wants from your test responses. This is determined somewhat by the type of test you will take, but often professors are looking for something specific. Sometimes they will tell you exactly what they are looking for—the personality differences between two literary characters, for example. But most of the time, you'll be on your own in this regard. To accommodate this situation, review your notes and identify themes and concepts the professor spent considerable time on, and places where lecture notes and readings overlap. These are all indications that the professor thinks that material is especially important and is likely to include it on the test.

Once you have identified what you need to study, review your notes and pertinent readings. Go back and rewrite your notes, creating a master study sheet just for this test. Make summary sheets of important information, flash cards of dates, facts, and people, and then shuffle them and quiz yourself.

Be certain to answer easy questions first. This will give you more time for the harder questions and may help jog your memory. Don't spend too much time on any one question. If it is proving to be difficult move on and come back when you have finished the other questions. Also, remember that there is never a prize for being the first person done with a test. You should not rush during a test, but if there is a time limit, keep an eye on the clock. If you finish early, go back and review everything. If you find yourself running out of time and know you will not finish, work on the questions with the highest point values or those that you know you will answer correctly.

When you get your graded test returned to you, go through it carefully. You want to find the answers you missed and relearn that material. You also want to make note of the items that surprised you. Why didn't you anticipate that material would be on the test? More importantly, why did the professor include that information on the test? The answers to these questions will help you better prepare for the next test.

**QUESTION?**

**What if you get nervous during tests?**
Some anxiety during tests is natural. If this happens to you take your mind off self-defeating thoughts, picture notes and rehearse key concepts, and take several slow deep breaths. Focus on the item in front of you instead of how you are doing overall. If anxiety is a recurring or overwhelming problem visit the counseling center for advice.

If you have been spending enough time studying throughout the course, and not just for the test, you should be able to take a test with confidence and do well. However, if you are not getting grades that reflect the work you put into the course then talk to the professor to get suggestions for what you could do differently. Remember, she also wants to see you succeed. If your professor is not available, find a tutor or other assistance, perhaps from the advising center or learning support center on campus. It is your responsibility to make changes if you want to improve, but don't get discouraged and give up. After all, you were admitted to your college because you have the potential to succeed there.

*Chapter 18*

# Research and Term Papers

While a test is usually completed in one class period, a term paper can seem to last forever. From developing your topic and doing research to writing it out and having it handed back to you full of red marks—the process can seem endless and disheartening. But the ability to do research and present findings in a professional manner is a foundation of the modern college education. The skills you gain during the research and writing process will serve you well for the rest of your life.

## *Choosing a Topic*

Your first task will be deciding on a topic for your research paper. Sometimes this will be assigned to you, but most of the time you'll have to propose one to your professor. You may also have to determine a particular viewpoint to pursue for your paper. Your research must be unbiased, but your professor may want you to examine the available material and reach your own conclusions. As such, you'll use your paper to support a particular argument or point of view.

When choosing a topic, consider several important factors. For example, how does the topic fit with the material you're covering in class? The advantage to picking a topic that is related to ongoing coursework is that you may have more resources available to you. Your textbook, syllabus, and even lecture notes may help you throughout the process. You can also choose a topic that is not directly covered by your class, which may be more interesting for you, but it still must have some connection to the subject matter of your class.

**QUESTION?**

**Should you pick a term paper topic that matches your professor's specialty?**
Many students shy away from this, feeling that they can never live up to the professor's expectations. However, professors take into account that you are an undergraduate, and they may be better able to help you find material if they are thoroughly familiar with your topic.

You also need to consider how much information is available on the topic you choose. For an introductory course, you probably want a topic that has been widely researched or discussed. This will give you a variety of sources to work with, and the sources are more likely to be available in any college library. For an upper-level course, such as one required for majors in your area of study, a widely researched topic can be a disadvantage. You will be expected to cover material more deeply, and too many sources may mean that you are never able to cover the topic in depth or that you are overwhelmed by the breadth of the topic.

# Outlines

By the time you finish high school, you may feel like you have completed endless paper outlines. Many high school students complain that outlines are unnecessary, and if they don't have to hand in an outline in advance many students won't create an outline until their final paper has been completed. In college your papers will have to be more complex and organized, and an outline is an important part of the process.

Before you can fill in your outline you must have a reasonable thesis statement. This is your central idea for the paper. It will act as a compass for your research and writing and will tie your entire outline together. A thesis statement should be simple and to the point. It should state what you are trying to prove or convey in your paper. Here are some sample thesis statements:

- Short-term memory has been widely studied but is not yet fully understood by modern psychologists.
- The political relationship between Cuba and the United States has been greatly affected by the activism of Cuban expatriates.
- The study of fruit flies has shown great potential in understanding human genetics.

Once you have a thesis statement, it's time to fill in your outline. The easiest parts of the outline are the introduction and conclusion. To start, jot down a few ideas of what you want to say in your introduction, including your thesis statement, and also write down a few lines to use in your conclusion. Then set these sections aside. The harder part of the outline is organizing your material to meet the requirements of the paper and to accurately reflect the research that you will complete. But for most papers, you will only need three or four main points. If you have more than that, consider grouping two or three as subsections of a slightly larger area. Each main point should have one to three interior points. Every point and interior point should support your thesis and lead to a reasonable conclusion.

When completed, your outline should clearly demonstrate your approach to the paper. Anyone should be able to look at this document and understand what points you are going to make and how you will support your thesis. Keep in mind that your outline can change as you conduct your research and complete your writing. You may find that an initial idea was wrong, or that there is information you did not anticipate. The outline is a guide, but it is not set in stone.

Think of your outline as a table of contents for your paper. It will show anyone, at a glance, what the paper will cover. Throughout the research and writing process, keep your outline where you can see it. Doing so will help you keep the big picture in mind, as well as help keep your thoughts organized.

## Getting Help from Your Professor

Your professor is another key resource to consider when working on your term paper. You can usually ask him for advice when you run into problems, and your professor may offer to look at your outline or a section of your paper and give you feedback. First, be sure that you understand your professor's expectations for the project. Does he want a review of the literature, or does he want you to support a particular argument? Are there particular sources he wants you to consult? What do you think is his purpose in giving this particular assignment? Understanding your professor's motivation may help guide your progress through a paper.

Once you're certain you understand your professor's expectations and have outlined your approach, sit down with him during his office hours and explain your plan. Your professor will be able to help you adjust your approach, if necessary, and you will have a better idea of what your professor is looking for in the research or paper. This will not necessarily guarantee you a better grade, but it will show your professor that you care about the assignment and the class.

Don't be reluctant to ask your professor for suggested sources. Part of the research process includes your ability to discover general sources that are available, but your professor may be willing to point you in the right direction or recommend some specialized resources. Remember that your professor is an expert researcher and thus an excellent resource for you.

Many professors will expect to see a rough draft before you have finished your paper. Although your professor is likely to make a variety of corrections and suggestions at this stage, this works to your advantage. You'll have a better paper in the end and will be writing to your professor's specific expectations. If your professor does not require a rough draft, ask her if she will look over what you have and give you some feedback before the deadline. Not only will this help you write the best possible paper, but it will also demonstrate to the professor that you are interested in the topic and are willing to learn.

**ALERT!**

Your professor will not do your research or write your paper for you. When approaching your professor, be sure to tell him first what ideas you are considering and what sources you have found. Only after you let him know that you are seriously working on the paper should you ask for suggestions or guidance.

## Research

Research is a fundamental part of the college experience, and is a strong requirement for obtaining most advanced degrees. While it will be time-consuming, it doesn't have to be difficult. As long as you allow yourself enough time to get your work done, you should be able to complete your research thoroughly and write an excellent paper.

The library is the place where you'll conduct most of your research. In your first semester of college, either during orientation or through a freshman seminar, you should have an orientation to the library. If that does not happen formally, visit the library on your own and ask the staff if there is an orientation available for new students. You may get an individual tour, join a group, or be given a recording that will allow for a self-guided tour. It may seem pointless to get an orientation, particularly if you have used a library before, but it is worth the time to find out precisely how your school's library works. This preliminary measure will save you time and energy every time you have to conduct research.

All colleges have a catalog of their holdings. Older catalogs are kept on cards that you manually sort through to find the items you are looking for. Most schools have placed their catalogs into searchable databases that save time and energy. With these systems, you're able to search by author, title, subject, or keyword. You're also likely to have access to databases that will search the holdings of other libraries. For example, Worldcat is an online database that lists the holdings of thousands of libraries. Your college probably has an exchange program with other schools, which enables you to order books and other sources from other libraries and receive them by mail.

**ALERT!**

If you are going to order something from another library you may have to wait several days for it to arrive. Taking this into account, you should order all interlibrary loan materials well in advance of your paper's due date. Ordering from another library may also include a nominal fee, so be certain that you really need the item you are ordering.

You will also be able to search the Internet for resources related to your topic. Internet searches may yield thousands of results, so be as specific as possible with your searches. You must also be cautious when finding information on the Internet. Almost anyone can post information on the Internet, so separating fact from opinion can be difficult.

It is very important to keep track of any source that you consult. You'll have to provide a citation each time you use someone else's ideas, and you'll likely have to include a list of the sources you used when you turn in your paper. Many professors also want to know what books and articles you read to prepare your paper even if you don't end up using those sources in your text. Many students use index cards to keep track of sources and quotes. If you use one index card per source, you can easily keep track of the sources you consult.

Your professor will have a preferred method of citing sources and will usually ask you to use a particular style guide. The *Chicago Manual of Style* and the *Associated Press Stylebook* are two examples of style guides. Your college bookstore will have the style guides most often used by professors. It is a good idea to purchase one of these books as a reference, especially if your major will require a lot of research and writing.

As you take notes from books, periodicals, and other sources take the time to note which source gave you each quote. Too many college students, while desperately writing their papers the night before it is due, find an excellent quote but can't remember which source it came from. Keeping your notes on index cards allows you to quickly write the source information on the reverse side of the card. You don't need to copy all of the source information if you already have that on another card, but writing down the author or title will save you a lot of time later on.

In addition to your college library, individual academic departments may maintain specialized libraries. An economics department, for example, may have its own library in the building where the professors have their offices. Here, you'll find more specific information, fewer people vying for the same resources, and perhaps computers to use while working on your paper.

Don't think of research as a one-time visit to the library or Internet. You'll probably have to make several trips to the library, place multiple orders for books from another library, and consult the Internet on more than one occasion. As you work on your first draft, you'll probably find that you need to find more information to support a particular point, or that a new point has emerged. If you expect these occurrences from the start, you'll be more flexible when things come up.

## Where to Start Writing

One of the most intimidating sights for a college student may be a blank piece of paper or the blinking cursor on an empty computer screen. You will likely sit at your desk, surrounded by notes and sources, only to find yourself wondering where to being. It will be difficult to choose an approach to the paper or a good place to start, but the key is to force yourself to begin. You can always revise your writing later.

**ALERT!**

Perhaps the most important error to avoid when writing a paper is plagiarism. Plagiarism occurs when you use other people's words without giving them credit. Whether you claim another's words as your own on purpose or by accident, the punishment will likely be the same. This offense could cause you to fail the assignment or even be suspended from your college. Be certain to give credit where it is due when using research in your paper.

Many students choose to start with the section they feel most or least confident about. Starting with the section you are most comfortable with allows you to get a lot of words out quickly and helps you get into the writing experience. Starting with the section you are dreading gets that section out of the way early and forces you to work hard from the start, making it easier for you to focus on the other sections later.

Another widely used approach is to start with the introduction or conclusion. Beginning at the opening of your paper allows you to ease into the subject matter just as your reader will. It also allows you to restate your thesis and decide where the paper needs to go. Beginning with the conclusion helps you focus on where the paper will leave the reader. If you are writing a persuasive paper you may especially benefit from beginning with your conclusion. Once you have determined your final point or message, you can organize the preceding material accordingly.

# Saving Your Work

Imagine that it's late at night and you're in a computer lab with dozens of other students. Except for the sound of typing, the room is silent. Pages of notes, heavily highlighted books, and photocopies of library materials surround each student as she works feverishly on a major project. Then, suddenly, there is a power surge; computers shut down and then reboot. You can picture the reaction in the room. Students might cry, shout, or simply stare at their computer screens in shock. Every year a technological failure or glitch causes students stress on every college campus. For this reason, you must take certain precautions to protect your work and your sanity.

When working on a computer, you must get in the habit of saving your work every five minutes or so. Most word processing programs have auto-save features, but it is also a good idea to save manually, in case the auto-save function becomes disabled. If you have trouble remembering to save your work, try setting an alarm on your watch to remind you to do so.

You also need to save multiple copies of your work. This may seem excessive at first, but if your computer crashes or you lose the disk with your paper on it, you'll be in a bad situation. You will still have to hand in your work on time, and most professors are unsympathetic to excuses. Save a copy to your hard drive and another copy to a CD. Some schools will give students access to a shared drive, which has several advantages. First, the drive is backed up regularly so that if there are any problems data can be recovered. Second, files from a shared drive can be accessed from any computer connected to the campus network. You can access your files from any computer on campus, and even your computer in your room. Saving a copy to a shared drive is highly advisable.

**QUESTION?**

**How long should you save copies of your paper?**
If you get an "A" on a paper, you might want to save the paper forever. In general, though, you should save one electronic copy and one hard copy of each paper for as long as you are in college. You never know when that old paper will come in handy for a future project.

## Polishing a Rough Draft

Once you have gotten your thoughts down on paper, it's time to take a break. Set your paper aside for a few hours or a full day and work on assignments for other classes or go get some exercise. Once you have had some time away from your writing, come back and read through your rough draft. The first things you want to look for are the main ideas and their adherence to your thesis statement. Questions you should ask yourself at this point include:

- Does the organization of the paper make sense?
- Do the ideas flow easily from one to another?
- Does each section support your thesis?
- Is any important information missing?
- Will a reader who is not familiar with the subject understand your points?

After you have answered these questions and made necessary adjustments, it's time to get out your red pen and go through your paper line by line, looking for spelling errors, poor sentence structure, and punctuation mistakes. Many computer word processing programs will automatically help you identify possible errors, but always trust your dictionary and style guide over the word processor. Read through your paper, perhaps reading it out loud or going through it backward, in order to find errors.

You should polish your paper several times before you turn it in. Each time you make a correction or incorporate new ideas into the paper reread it, searching for errors or confusing sections. By the time you finish you may feel that you are able to recite your paper verbatim, but this will help ensure that you have done a thorough job. This complete understanding of your topic will also come in handy in class discussions or during one-on-one meetings with your professor.

## Writing Centers and Proofreaders

After you have made all your corrections and are happy with your paper, you need to get an objective opinion. Your roommate or other friends may be willing to read through your paper and give you suggestions. However, friends may not want to give you criticism and they may not know enough about writing to notice some of your errors. While friends can tell you if the general ideas make sense you need to head elsewhere for objective assistance.

If you enjoy writing, you might look for a work-study job in the writing center. After some training, you'll be able to use your skills to help other students become better writers. In addition to the satisfaction that comes from helping someone, you'll make some money. You may also get good topic ideas for future papers and make friends with the students you assist.

Most colleges have a writing center available to all students. The staff members at the writing center are usually other students trained to help their peers develop writing skills and achieve their goals for each paper. However, these students will not write a paper for you. They will point out positive and negative aspects of your writing, from good arguments to poor sentence structure. Staff may even suggest that you rethink an entire section or rework your thesis statement.

When you visit the writing center, be prepared for constructive criticism. Keep in mind that you and the staff share a common goal: To make your paper as strong as possible. When you leave the writing center, you'll probably have a bunch of errors to correct. However, if your professor found these errors in your final draft, your grade would likely be lower. Take the writing center staff's recommendations to heart, treat them as advice that you may still choose to disregard, and revise your paper at least one last time after your visit. You will also have the option to visit the same staff member with a corrected draft a few days later. If the writing center staff can no longer find errors in your paper, and once you are satisfied with your work, chances are it is ready to be turned in.

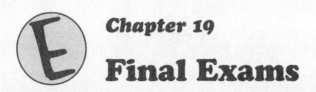

## Chapter 19
# Final Exams

The term "final" in "final exam" can mean one of two things. At the end of a challenging semester spent dedicating yourself to succeeding in your class, you may consider a final exam a possibility for failure. But if you have prepared well for the exam, you may consider it a chance to shine and raise your final grade in the class. In truth, a final exam is what you make of it. You can do quite well on almost any final exam with good study habits and a little extra preparation, and you'll still have time to socialize with your friends.

## *Exam Format*

If you want to truly succeed on your final exam, you need to know more than just the subject matter covered in your course—you need to know what type of exam your professor will give. This will determine how you study and will tell you a lot about what your professor is looking for from your final exam.

Cumulative final exams, covering the entire semester of material, are relatively common. While this is often intimidating to new students, this format can work in your favor. A cumulative exam generally covers more material but cannot cover it deeply. You must understand the general concepts covered in class, how they are interconnected, and be able to tie them to a few specific examples. Contrary to popular belief, cumulative exams don't necessarily require more studying; they just require a different approach.

Time management is crucial when it comes to exams. One approach is to divide the allotted exam time by the number of questions you have to answer. Don't exceed that amount of time per question, and return to incomplete items only if you have time at the end. It is better to at least partially answer all questions than to leave several questions blank.

If your exam is not cumulative, you'll likely be tested on the second half or last quarter of the material covered in the class. However, the material covered at the beginning of the semester will usually be a foundation for what will appear on the exam, so don't put that knowledge out of your mind. A noncumulative final exam is likely to cover a few items in depth, so take this into consideration while you study.

You'll need to know if your final exam will be based primarily on material covered in class lectures, found in required readings, mentioned in class discussions, or all three. A professor is likely to tell you that you should be familiar with all of these; after all, the professor wants you to learn as much as possible about this particular topic. Ask your professor for these types of information, but be prepared to ask other people as well. Students who have taken a class with this professor are a good resource, especially if they have taken the specific class that you are taking.

## Tips for Essay Exams

If your final exam will consist of essay or short answer questions, you'll almost certainly have to explain concepts covered in class. Preparation for these types of exams should include reviewing vocabulary; using the correct words will help the professor know that you understand the subject matter. Also, go back through your notes and identify themes or sections that your professor lectured about at length. The more time a professor spends on a particular concept the more likely it is to appear on your final exam.

During essay exams, always outline your answers on a scrap piece of paper before entering them into the exam booklet. A well-organized essay will be easier for you to write and for the professor to read. Make certain to include a brief introduction and concise summary. Your thesis may simply be a variation on the exam question or it may need to be a little more developed.

Essay and short answer exams can be tricky if you don't know what your professor is looking for from each answer. Fortunately, most professors will be clear about what they want from you. Look for key words that will direct your response to each question. Examples of such key words and their instructions to you are:

- Compare: highlight similarities and differences
- Describe: give an account
- Discuss: present the different facets
- Summarize: give the main points briefly
- Evaluate: review the advantages and limitations
- Trace: follow the course or development
- Interpret: provide the meaning
- Illustrate: use an example to explain a point

After you have finished your essay or short answer, take a moment to proofread what you wrote. Look for spelling, grammar, and punctuation errors. These seemingly small items will make a difference in your grade. Even if your professor will not deduct points for such errors, she will notice which answers are easy to read. If she has to stop to figure out your grammar or spelling, it will detract from the point you are trying to make.

## Tips for Multiple-Choice Exams

Multiple-choice exams have the reputation of being easier for students. After all, isn't it easier if you can simply guess the answer? Students who approach multiple-choice exams with this point of view often find that they have underestimated their professor and their class. Multiple-choice questions can cover just as much material as essay questions, and they force you to make educated guesses if you don't know the answer.

These exams will usually include vocabulary definitions and specific facts. Many students assume that a general idea of the course material will be sufficient on a multiple-choice exam. However, there is no substitute for thorough knowledge, and diligent studying will pay off. If you are having trouble with a question, consider the following tips; however, keep in mind that these are only tips and not necessarily rules:

- If the answer doesn't fit the grammatical structure of the question it is probably incorrect
- Vague answers tend to be incorrect
- If two alternatives are opposites, one of them is probably correct
- If two choices overlap, both are probably wrong (if there is only one correct answer)
- If two items are correct then "all of the above" is probably correct
- "Always" and "never" tend to appear in incorrect answers
- Correct answers sometimes repeat some of the terms in the question
- If two choices mean essentially the same thing, both are probably wrong

**Where do you start on a multiple-choice exam?**
Always read through the whole exam before starting to answer questions. Then choose to start with the section that will be easiest for you. This will give you the confidence of having completed a section or two well before spending extra time on more challenging areas.

## *Tips for Presentations*

Some professors might assign a presentation in place of a final exam. The structures of such presentations varies greatly from class to class, however, a few tips will help you, no matter what the subject matter. For example, always dress nicely for your presentation. This will make a difference, even if your professor doesn't specifically grade for it. Also, get a good night's sleep before your presentation. If you start yawning halfway through your remarks, you'll lose your audience. And as always, there is no substitute for thoroughly knowing the subject of your presentation. You need to be prepared to explain or demonstrate what you are talking about and answer questions about that topic on the spot.

The biggest mistake students make with presentations is failing to rehearse prior to the presentation. Whether you rehearse in front of friends or just in front of a mirror be sure to go through your entire presentation at least once. Also, practice standing and talking naturally, using helpful (but not distracting) hand gestures, and referencing (but not reading) your note cards. It is also imperative that you practice using any visual aids included in your presentation. And if you are using a computer, be certain that you have a back-up plan in case the technology fails at a critical moment.

The final, and perhaps most important tip for making presentations is to be confident. Even if you are uncertain about your material you need to speak as though you have no doubts. Your confident appearance will help ease your nerves and convince your audience, your professor, and yourself that you are thoroughly prepared for the presentation.

# A Quick Guide to Studying

Studying for a final exam is a bit different from the studying you did during the regular semester. On the one hand, you have the luxury of a more open time schedule and can devote as much time as you want to a particular exam. On the other hand, you have a lot of material to cover, and if your exam is worth a significant portion of your final class grade, the pressure may be increased as well.

You need to study concepts repeatedly. Even after you have learned particular material and can recite it without error, continue to include it in your studying. This sort of repeated learning will help solidify the concepts in your mind and can keep you from drawing a blank when you get to the exam.

Your professor will tell you how to study for the final exam, but it is up to you to listen to and remember this information. A few professors will suggest that you focus on a textbook, class notes, or a particular concept covered in class. Most of the time, you must interpret the signs your professor has given throughout the semester. If the professor relied heavily on the textbook during class discussions, the final is likely to be based on that material. If the professor lectured extensively, much of the exam may come from lecture notes. Professors spend the most time teaching and reviewing the information they feel is the most important. This is the information you can expect to see on the exam.

Your studying should begin with a review of your class notes. Look for themes and patterns in material the professor covered. Also, look for sections you found confusing and devote some time to going over them again. Use index cards to isolate important points in your notes, writing down key phrases or concepts that you can easily review later.

Similarly, review any textbooks that were used in class. Pay attention to the places where the textbook and the professor's lectures overlap. Look at sections you highlighted and consider taking notes on the material in your textbook. A collection of index cards with key concepts or chapter thesis statements can be a useful tool later.

One of the most valuable study tools you have is your old tests and quizzes from the class. You can learn three basic things from these materials:

- Your professor's preferred format for exams
- The concepts your professor focuses on
- The material you struggled with in the past

After you have reviewed these points, you should have a strong idea of what areas to focus on in your studying. Focusing on these issues will help you make the best possible final impression on your professor and also ensure that nothing surprises you on the day of the exam.

**FACT**

Index cards can help you organize your thoughts, be used as flashcards, and even act as bookmarks. They are inexpensive and easy to use for a quick review while waiting in line or for friends to arrive for a meal. And they are small enough to fit easily in your bookbag or pockets—just be careful not to lose them.

## Review Sessions

After all the reviewing you have done on your own, why bother with a review session? And aren't review sessions really meant for the students who haven't studied? Actually, these misconceptions can lead you to missing out on one of the most valuable study tools available at college. Beyond your individual study time, review sessions are the best way to prepare for your final exam.

Many review sessions will be organized or approved by your professor. While the professor usually does not attend these sessions, she may send a graduate student, teaching assistant, or tutor to lead the session. The person in charge of these sessions will be familiar with both the subject matter and the professor, making him a very valuable resource. During the session, you'll have the chance to go through key concepts and materials, ask questions about points that are unclear, and hear the questions that other students have.

Review sessions fall into two categories: lecture and discussion. Lecture sessions still give you the opportunity to ask questions but move at a quicker pace. Discussion sessions give everyone a chance to express their thoughts about the topic and can be very useful when preparing for final exams in an essay format. The more ideas you have for an essay exam the better.

Sometimes review sessions will be arranged independently of the professor. Such sessions can be very helpful or a big waste of your time. If you have completed your other studying, try to attend these sessions and see what they have to offer. If a group of students are gathered to talk seriously about the class material, you are likely to benefit from the session. On the other hand, if a group of students meet with no set purpose, you probably won't benefit much from the experience.

After the review session has ended, make a list of the items that were covered. Compare that list to the outline or list that you created based on your notes and textbooks. If the two lists are very similar, you're in good shape. If several of the topics covered in the review session don't appear in your own private study notes, you should spend extra time on these areas. Finally, combine the two lists to create a master list that can serve as the basis of further studying.

## Study Blocks

During final exam week, you will not have classes to attend. Your schedule will appear to be wide open and this can lull you into a sense of complacency. You have lots of time, so why be too formal about your schedule? However, the free time is an illusion and you need to be deliberate about how you approach your studying during this week. Study blocks are a popular method for many students. These are significant periods of study that allow you to thoroughly and deeply review subject matter for a single class. If you treat a study block schedule like a schedule of classes and don't miss any, this method can prove very effective.

Your daily study schedule should always begin with a good breakfast. Once you have eaten, you can decide how you will spend your day. For most students, the morning hours will constitute a single study block. During this block you may take quick breaks, perhaps to take a quick walk or grab a snack. However, you don't want to engage yourself too deeply in other activities. You must return to your study block without having lost your focus.

**ALERT!**

Your old time-management schedule will not work during a final exam week—you will need to make a new schedule during this time. Fill in the blank schedule with each exam you have and meal times. Then schedule study blocks around those items, being specific about what class you will study for in each block. Post the schedule where you can see it and make sure that you stick to it.

Meals provide nice natural breaks in your study blocks. They give you the opportunity to get away from studying for a little while and socialize with friends. For some students, meals are a good time to compare notes with other students in your class. Sitting together as a group and discussing what you're each reviewing might be helpful. The more trouble you're having with the material, the more you will need to consider using meals as study times.

Your afternoons and evenings may contain one or two study blocks each. You need to make sure you're giving each class enough study time as you prepare for the exam. Keep in mind that your exams will be spread out over the week. Focus your studying on the classes that are most difficult and deal with the exams chronologically.

## *Practice Tests*

Taking a test is not altogether different from playing a sport. Proper exercise and practice will help you perform well in a game, and plenty of rest and thorough studying will ensure success on an exam. Practice tests are the final piece necessary to succeed on a final exam. Once you have a good grasp of the material that will be covered on the final exam, you're ready for some more advanced preparation.

Start with the outline or list of key concepts that you have created from your notes, textbooks, and review sessions. This is the material you think the professor will cover on the exam. From that create a mini-test, using the format that your professor is likely to use. You probably don't need to write full essays, but creating a quick outline for each answer will tell you if you are prepared for an essay exam. You can also create your own multiple-choice test or vocabulary review.

Talk to students who have taken classes with your professor to find out what the exam might be like. A professor's style is usually consistent, regardless of the class she is teaching. However, a student who has had your class with a different professor may not give you accurate advice. Solicit advice primarily from people who know your professor well.

It's important that you quiz yourself but you may also benefit from working with a partner at this stage. You and your partner can each create a practice test for one another. Going back and forth like this will help you learn the material thoroughly and get another student's perspective on some of your answers. However, be selective when choosing this study partner. You want to work with someone who is as serious about studying as you are, and you don't want to be doing all the work for both of you.

## *Physical Preparation*

Think of a test as a performance for your mind. You already know that your body does not perform as well when it is worn out. Whether you are an athlete or an actress, you know that you need to exercise your body appropriately in order to be prepared when it comes time to take the field or go on stage. Similarly, when it is time to take a final exam, your mind must be appropriately prepared for the challenge.

**ALERT!**

Don't forget to eat nutritious foods while you are studying. Foods high in protein will help your brain function better. On the day of your exam, allow yourself enough time to eat a good breakfast without rushing. If your exam is scheduled for midmorning or midafternoon, have a breakfast bar or some other quick, high-protein snack before the exam.

The first and most obvious thing you need to do is get a good night's sleep prior to your exam. If you have been studying diligently and intelligently, you can set your books and notes aside in favor of a good seven or eight hours of sleep. You may find it hard to turn off your brain, with thoughts of key concepts or important dates running through your head. But getting enough rest will pay off when you arrive in the classroom for your test. A rested mind will be able to create better essays, pick up on key words more quickly, and adapt to any surprises that appear.

It's also important to avoid burning yourself out. Though it may sound contradictory, deserting your study materials from time to time is a good idea. An evening of intense studying should be interspersed with several breaks that involve thoroughly relaxing activities. Take thirty minutes to watch a sitcom, or a little bit of time to take a walk around campus. Since you'll have to eat, make your meal a study break and leave your notes in your room. Find a few friends to join you for a quick meal or snack and talk about anything except your exams. When you return to your studies, you'll feel refreshed and your mind will be prepared to absorb more important information.

## Chapter 20

# Internships and Summer Jobs

For most college students, summer is the longest break of the academic year. It's a long enough break that even after a vacation, you'll still have to find something productive to do with the remainder of your time. However, after a couple of years of college, the job you had during high school will no longer suffice. It probably won't help you build your resume, and it may not pay as much as other opportunities. An internship or more focused summer job will help you pursue your career goals and will provide you with valuable life experience.

## *Make Meaningful Money*

As an upper-level college student, your summer experience must include two things. First, it must be meaningful. You must do something more than you have done in past summers, something that will further your academic or career interests. At the end of the summer, your resume should be stronger and you should be a more attractive candidate to a future employer. Second, you need to make money. College expenses extend far beyond tuition, meals, and books. After a year of college, you'll have an idea of how much money you need to earn during the summer. Ideally, you'll also be building a savings account to help you get established after graduation.

Combining these two goals may be difficult. For example, you may find the perfect internship, one that gives you good experience and connections in your future career field. However, the internship may be unpaid, and you'll virtually be a volunteer. In such cases, you'll need to earn money with a second job outside of your internship, and finding a job that has the right hours might be difficult. In such situations, students often find the summer busier than the school year. However, these experiences will pay off in the end.

The ideal situation is a paid internship. A paid internship gives you the experience you want and a paycheck to cover your needs. However, be prepared for that paycheck to be small. A second job may be a good idea, even if the internship is paid. The more money you can earn in the summer the better.

If you have to get a job just for money, whether or not you have an internship, work hard to find something more meaningful than you have had in past summers. Look for positions that involve supervising others or taking on significant responsibilities. Be assertive when interviewing, and point out any experiences you had at college that might be helpful. Your campus job may have taught you new skills, or a leadership position in an organization may impress a prospective employer. Also, emphasize that you are responsible and committed, and that you are looking for more than just a paycheck. Throughout your experience, keep in mind that whatever job you take can result in a valuable job reference for use the following summer or after graduation.

**What is an internship?**
Internships are experiences that connect work site experience with academic studies. You may be able to get academic credit for an internship, or you may receive a salary or stipend. Internships are often available during the summer, as well as the academic year. For more information about internships, check with your college's career center.

If you're not able to find a meaningful job or internship for the summer, look for service opportunities. Volunteering to work with a local shelter or hospital can be extremely rewarding and translate into an excellent entry on your resume. These experiences can profoundly affect how you view the world and give you a sense of accomplishment. Consider volunteering with a local youth program as well. Serving as a coach or instructor can be a lot of fun, is good for your resume, and will give you the opportunity to improve a young person's life.

## Professors as Resources

When looking for summer jobs, one of the most overlooked resources is the college professor. Your professors had to spend years in college and also had to find some way to pay for all of that education. In addition to scholarships, they had to find good summer jobs that either paid well or furthered their academic interests. Some of your professors may have had particularly interesting summer jobs, such as working at a national park or at a major museum. Their experiences may result in new ideas or very good contacts for your summer job search.

Early in the spring semester, take a few minutes to think about the professors you most enjoy or respect. These may be professors you have had for classes, heard lecture outside of class, had as an advisor, or otherwise know about. Talk to each of them about what they did for summer jobs, what you hope to do, and what options might benefit your career goals. Be open to new ideas that your professors suggest, and don't be shy about asking for their help in securing a good summer job.

Ask your professor about her best summer work experience. She will enjoy talking about the experience, and you may gain a great idea for your own summer. You will also build a better relationship with your professor. Even if the idea isn't related to your career field, it may be valuable in other ways.

Professors may also have good connections for summer internship opportunities. They may be working on special projects themselves—on campus or at another site. Perhaps they have a friend at another college who needs a summer intern with your capabilities. And professors might know of professionals in your desired career field who host interns each summer. If you know what you want to do after graduation, whether it's graduate school or a particular career, approach a professor in that field and ask for her assistance in helping you find an appropriate internship.

## Career Center

Your campus career center is an obvious place to go when searching for internships. Some career centers even have counselors who specialize in internships. Most career centers will maintain a book of the most popular internships for students at that school. The same information may be available on the career center's Web site. If you don't find the type of internship that you are looking for with these resources, ask a career counselor about other lists or ways of searching for internships. There are a variety of guides for specific fields, such as human rights, environmental work, and sports.

The career center can do more than just help you find an internship. The counselors can help you figure out the best way to approach the internship sponsor. You may need to go through a formal process or contact a particular person at the host agency. There may also be etiquette for making the initial contact, and the host agency is bound to have specific questions for you that go beyond your motivation for the internship. Your career center will help you prepare for all of these situations.

If your internship will be for academic credit, the career counselor or your academic advisor can help you work out the necessary details. You'll need an official faculty sponsor and will probably have to complete some papers or keep a journal in order to receive credit for your work. There may be some additional forms to complete in order to have an internship count for academic credit, and you may need to use specific wording if you want the internship to fill an academic requirement.

**FACT**

Working through your career center will be helpful in some subtle ways. Your career counselor will know you well, and will thus be better able to help you. You'll also be able to systematically build a superior resume since the career counselor will know what you did each summer, what you learned from your experiences, and what your goals are.

The career center is a frequently overlooked place to go when looking for a summer job. If this office can help students find a job after graduation, why can't the staff also assist with jobs for the summer? While this is not one of its primary missions, your career center is already set up with many of the resources necessary to find a good summer job. For example, companies may post summer job openings at your career center. The career center can help you put together a resume targeting your desired job and will likely help you prepare for the interview. Your career counselor will also be able to help you revise your resume after the summer job ends so that you can highlight your experiences and make yourself more attractive to future employers.

## Alumni Office

Many students perceive the alumni office as serving only those people who have graduated from college. In many cases, this is not true. Most of an alumni office's work is with graduates, but they have many resources and opportunities for undergraduates as well. It's worth your time to visit your campus alumni office, or look at its site on the Internet, to see what services it can offer you as an undergraduate.

Alumni offices often facilitate volunteer networks of professionals willing to speak with and mentor undergraduates. For example, if you're considering a career as a journalist, check the volunteer listing and locate several alumni who are working in journalism as reporters or editors. Once you have their contact information, you can ask them questions about how their education prepared them for the job, how the job diverged from their expectations, and what would have made their job search easier. Many times, you'll be able to set up a visit to see each alumnus at his job, giving you more education and strengthening the connection between you and the alumnus.

Alumni offices sometimes work in conjunction with career services or other campus offices to set up internships for students. This is an excellent opportunity for an undergraduate to work in her desired field and be mentored by an alumnus. The alumnus is likely to look out for you during the internship, give you advice, and help ensure that you have a good experience. He will be proud that a student from his college is working hard for his company, and the work you do will reflect well on him, too.

One reason that alumni work with undergraduates is their passion for the college. They valued their experience at the college and want to help other students. After you work with an alumnus, send him a postcard depicting a scene from the campus. If the experience was particularly helpful, consider sending a souvenir from the bookstore along with a thank you note.

Keep in touch with alumni that you meet through internships or volunteer networks. Once you've graduated, they may be able to help you network your way into your first job. Some fields are smaller than they seem, and your alumni contact may know the person who is interviewing you even if their companies are on opposite sides of the country. The alumnus may also be willing to serve as a job reference for you, and because they can speak the language of your desired career field, have established themselves as successful professionals, and have a connection to your school they can be powerful references.

At some point, you'll probably see signs around campus advertising the alumni office's annual phone-a-thon. This is the period where volunteers, usually students, call alumni to solicit donations. This actually represents a good opportunity for you and your friends. If you volunteer to be a caller during this program, you could earn some money and make connections with professionals in your field. Some colleges give prizes for the student who is able to raise the most money over the course of the phone-a-thon. In addition, you will get to answer alumni questions about what is going on around campus and what activities you enjoy most. At best, you will be able to connect with a few alumni and perhaps begin a relationship that will help you after college.

## *Professional Organizations*

Some professional organizations will sponsor internships for college students. This benefits the organization in a variety of ways. They are able to recruit young people to be members in their organization, to serve their current members, and to help train future leaders in their field. These organizations sometimes act as a clearinghouse for internship opportunities in the field. Member companies submit their openings to the professional organization, and the organization takes on the responsibility of soliciting and screening applicants.

**QUESTION?**

**How do you find professional organizations in your field?**
Ask someone who is currently working in the field in which you are interested. Family, professors, and alumni can all point you in the right direction as well. And keep your eye out for professions that have multiple professional organizations; pursuing opportunities with all of them is often an effective strategy.

Both the National Association of Student Personnel Administrators (NASPA) and the American College Personnel Association (ACPA) are examples of professional organizations that sponsor internships. They have established well-regarded programs for graduate and undergraduate students who want to work in higher education administration. Students who participate in these internships get to work on another college campus, usually receive a broad range of experiences, and gain excellent entries for their resumes. These students also have the opportunity to network in their career field and usually come away with an outstanding reference to use when they begin a job search.

## Reflections on Your Experience

In grade school, many students spend the first day of school talking about what they did for summer vacation. Some students have to write short essays about their experiences. In college, the experience is similar but the reasons are different. When you are putting together your next resume, the career counselor is going to ask you what you did for the summer and what you learned from the experience. Your academic advisor may ask you the same thing. And friends are going to ask you what you did during the summer, even if you communicated with them periodically over the previous few months.

If you have a summer internship or are working with a volunteer organization, it is worthwhile to keep a daily or weekly journal. Writing down a few sentences on a regular basis can help you recall important events and demonstrate to yourself how much you learned from the experiences. If you worked a job primarily for the money, keep a copy of the job description and make notes of additional responsibilities you had. At the end of the summer, no matter what type of experience you had, take some time to write down what you learned from the summer and how you think it benefited you.

When career counselors or advisors ask you about the summer, you want to have a thorough and interesting answer to give. However, if your answer isn't polished these people will help you sort through what you did and what it all means. They can also help you make connections between your summer experiences, your academic work, and your career goals.

When friends ask what you did for the summer, you want to have a better answer than "nothing." This casual approach will never be as impressive as a story about a trip you took to Africa with a professor, or an internship at a well-known radio station. While summer experiences should not create competition amongst your friends, you will have more to share and get excited about if you have each done something meaningful during your break from college. Allow your friends' experiences to motivate you, and relate your own experiences in a way that will inspire others.

*Chapter 21*

# Right Plan, Wrong School

Perhaps you get to college and realize that the school isn't right for you. The classes may be interesting, but the majors may not fit your career plans. Perhaps the school's sports are fun, but the social scene isn't. Or maybe a college will turn out to be too far from your family home. College is probably still the answer for you in this case; the challenge now lies in finding and transferring to the right college.

## *Why Transfer?*

There are both good and bad reasons to transfer schools. Unfortunately, it's hard to distinguish between good and bad reasons in the midst of a difficult time. The decision to transfer can be emotionally stressful for you and your family, and it can also be expensive. However, if your reasons for transferring are sound, in the long run this decision will be worth every difficult moment and every expense incurred.

Good reasons to transfer include insufficient academic programs, unmanageable cost, or a changing family situation. After arriving on campus, some students discover a career interest they had not considered before. However, the school may not offer a major that will help a student achieve that career. The good news is that now these students know exactly what to look for in another college.

For some students, usually those who head to college far away from home, things at home will change while they are at school. A parent may lose a job, or a family member may become seriously ill. These situations may present a good reason to transfer so that the student can be closer to family or live at home and help in some way. However, some of these circumstances are short-term problems and all a student will need to do is take a semester off of college. Before deciding to transfer for these reasons, have a long conversation with your family as well as an academic advisor or college counselor.

Bad reasons to transfer out of a college include poor roommate relations, homesickness, and missing a boyfriend or girlfriend back home. These are all temporary issues that can be fixed relatively quickly. In fact, transferring usually doesn't fix these issues; it just moves the problem from one college to another. Students with these types of difficulties should seek assistance from an RA, a college counselor, and family members. Often the key to working through these problems is finding an activity to become involved with. This will give the student something fun to focus on and help him forget his unhappiness.

The time a student transfers is also important. The general rule of thumb is to transfer prior to the third year of college. Up to that point, students may be able to transfer many classes to the new college and not fall behind in their progress toward graduation. Not all credits will transfer and students may have to take an extra semester or some summer classes in order to stay on their initial graduation timeline. But transferring after three years almost guarantees an extra year of college.

**ALERT!**

There are many academic paths to specific careers. For example, salespeople may have undergraduate degrees in economics, business, communications, or math. Even lawyers, who need specialized advanced degrees, can have undergraduate degrees in a wide variety of fields. Before deciding to transfer because of a major, be certain to speak with an advisor or a career counselor. Your major may still work, even if your career goals have changed.

Transferring after one semester usually doesn't give a student enough time to know what truly went wrong at the college. If she hasn't identified and worked through the difficult issues is she setting herself up to repeat the same mistakes in a new setting? Transferring after one semester can also be difficult because students don't have much time to search for a new school, get applications in, and make campus visits. Some schools may not have many spaces for midyear transfers. Students should stay at their first college for a full academic year, if possible.

## How to Transfer

Transferring is very different from the initial search for a school. Students who are transferring should have a much better idea of exactly what they are looking for. However, for most students, transferring still involves a significant search and visits to potential schools. Even if students are considering schools they have applied to previously, it will be necessary to ask new questions and examine those schools more closely the second time around.

The first step for a student who wants to transfer is to make a list of what he is looking for in a new school. Students should focus on what has caused them to want to transfer, such as specific majors offered by a college, as well as on preferences that have changed. For example, some students will start at a large college and decide that they really want a small campus. Other search criteria will remain the same for students who are transferring, such as a school's location or cost. Once a list is complete, start finding colleges that meet the new requirements. Some initial college options may still be viable choices, but there are hundreds of colleges that students have not considered. Some time in the library with a college guidebook or using online services is advisable. The second search for colleges should take considerably less time, since the student has a better concept of what he needs from a college.

An overlooked resource for students who want to transfer is the high school guidance counselor. This person already knows the student and has a good grasp of colleges. The guidance counselor can also serve as an excellent reference for the student, focusing on long-range high school achievements and potential instead of a short-lived commitment to a college.

Next, the student needs to contact potential new schools and find out what specifically is required of transfer applicants. Most schools have a separate application process for potential transfer students. A transcript of college work completed at the former school will be required and sometimes a statement from a dean or discipline system administrator indicating that the student is in good standing with the current college will also be requested. Poor grades or some disciplinary infractions will not necessarily keep a student from transferring, but admissions counselors want to have a good idea of what kind of student they are considering. Students who have poor grades or disciplinary records should submit an additional essay detailing the difficulties they had and explaining why these problems won't occur at the new school.

When a student has narrowed down the list of new schools to two or three, it's time to speak with an admissions counselor, preferably during a campus visit. The questions a student asks at this time should be more focused than during the initial college search. Students will have a better idea of their particular needs and what they are looking for in a college. They can ask questions about campus resources, social life, and college expectations. It's also a very good idea to request time to speak privately with a student from the college. A current student will speak more candidly about her experiences at the college.

**QUESTION?**

**How should you answer questions about what went wrong at a first college?**

These questions should be answered as honestly as possible, but without blaming other people. Focus on what you can control and change at the new school. Admitting that you made mistakes and want a chance to start over is perfectly acceptable.

During the interview with a potential new college, you can expect to be asked more specific questions than during the initial college search. The admissions counselor will expect you to know more about your goals and aspirations, to better understand college life, and to be even more serious about this search. You'll be asked why you want to transfer and you might be asked what went wrong at the first school. The admissions counselors want students to be successful at the new school, but they also want to know that the student has made the decision to transfer only after careful consideration and several attempts to resolve any difficulties.

## Keeping Grants and Scholarships

Upon transferring, you'll obviously lose any financial assistance provided by your first college. However, other financial assistance will often be transferable. It's up to you to direct the right questions to the right people and make certain that any portable financial aid—aid that can be used at any school—comes with you when you transfer.

As with the initial college search, the best place to start is with the financial aid office at the new school. The staff there will be best suited to advise you about how to transfer loans and grants from outside sources. For example, federal financial aid will be portable, but you will have to file paperwork to ensure that the money goes to the new school. Also, if the new school costs more or less than the first school the amount of federal aid that you qualify for will change.

Remember that financial aid involves a lot of paperwork and deadlines. You must provide your new school with copies of income tax statements, a complete FAFSA form, and any additional information requested by the new school. If something unfamiliar is requested, call the financial aid office at the new school for clarification.

While speaking with the financial aid officer at the new school it is a very good idea to inquire about college-sponsored grants or scholarships. Just as in the initial college search, the new school will have specific aid opportunities for students who meet specific criteria. The financial aid officer will have the most information about these opportunities and can advise the transferring student about what is available and how to apply for it.

You will also have to speak with community organizations, corporations, or foundations that provided you with grants or scholarships. If the aid is transferable to the new school, often a student will only have to send a letter notifying the organization of the change in schools. This is a good time to include a note of thanks for the continued support of each organization.

## Starting Anew with an Advantage

The first time a student heads to college represents a chance to start over, to break away from the image he had in high school, and to explore new things. When transferring, a student can do the same thing, only he can do it more intelligently and with considerably less effort. To begin with, the student should already have a good idea of who he is and who he wants to be. He should have learned not to try to impress others or appear popular. If these were mistakes made at the first school, transferring is a way to begin again.

The student who is transferring has also learned about time management and the college lifestyle. While all other new students will be experimenting with time management, the transfer student can get down to business right away. He will also have a good idea of what activities are most rewarding and where to find the social scene that is most appealing. College campuses are similar, so the transfer student only has to learn the names of new places before heading out and finding the lifestyle he wants.

Transfer students have another advantage over new students and sometimes returning students who have not transferred. Transfer students tend to be a little bit more serious about their college experience. Because they have had an experience at another college, transfer students can better appreciate the advantages of their new school, and they are often more committed to making the college experience successful. Though initial awkwardness may make things difficult, it will certainly be temporary.

**FACT**

Transferring to a new school does not exclude you from leadership opportunities in campus organizations. In fact, you'll have the advantage of having seen how things can be done differently. The key is to get involved in those organizations right away and to not be shy about wanting to be a leader. Your prior college experience may make you a valuable candidate for several leadership positions.

## Staying in Touch with Professors

Students who decide to transfer schools may have developed good relationships with one or two professors at their first schools. This may be an initial academic advisor, a freshman seminar instructor, or a professor of a class that was particularly interesting. The longer a student is at a college, the deeper and more meaningful the relationship with the professor. However, transferring to a new school does not mean that a student's association with a professor is over. In fact, professors are often glad to stay in touch with transferring students.

Before transferring, you should sit down and talk with the professors whom you have become close to. Explaining why you are transferring is a good start to the conversation, though by this point you and your professor may have already had such a conversation. Next, you should ask if you can stay in touch with the professor. There may be a shared area of interest, such as a particular author or a research project, that can sustain the relationship. Most of the time, the professor will be glad to continue such a relationship with a student. Professors are in the education field because they like to inspire a passion for learning in their students. Your enthusiasm will only help the situation.

Keeping in touch with particular professors can also be specifically beneficial to you. Professors from a previous college can still serve as references for jobs or graduate schools. They can also serve as mentors and advisors, and are often happy to do so even when you are at another institution. While former professors can't advise you on requirements at a new college, they can help direct a job search, provide networking opportunities, and perhaps even collaborate on research projects. These relationships are well worth maintaining.

## Maintaining Friendships

College is an intense experience for students, and even after one semester most students have built very meaningful friendships. Transferring is often difficult in part because it means leaving the friends a student has come to value so much. The longer a student is at a school, the greater the number of friends and the depth of the friendships. Most of the time, these friends will mean more to a student than many of the friends she had in high school. However, you should not let these friendships stop you from pursuing your goals at another institution. There are ways to maintain these friendships, even from another campus.

Students don't become friends because they attend the same college. Certainly the campus serves as a common meeting place, but they choose to become friends because of shared interests, values, and memories. Upon graduating college, these friendships will endure. Things are no different for a transferring student. This student is leaving the college before his friends, but the friendships should remain.

**What if old friends don't return calls or letters right away?**
Don't read into slow responses from friends at a previous college. They are busy pursuing an active social life and academic success, just as you are. Some will be quicker to respond than others. But don't let this get you down. Go out and pursue new friendships in the meantime.

The transferring student should leave his first college with an address book full of contact information from his friends. And as soon as he knows his contact information at his new school, he should send that information out. E-mail and instant message services make it easy for students to stay in touch, even if their schools are far apart. It's also common for students to visit their old schools, or for them to host their old friends at their new schools. Break periods are another opportunity to reunite with friends, whether it's on a big vacation or back at someone's home.

The experience at a new school will include new friends. A student who has transferred should reach out and make as many new friends as possible. This does not mean that she is replacing old friendships; she is simply acquiring new ones. A person never knows which of her college friends will be the most meaningful during her lifetime. You may end up in the same city as a friend you had at your first college after you've both graduated. Therefore, the effort to stay in touch with friends from the first college is well worth it.

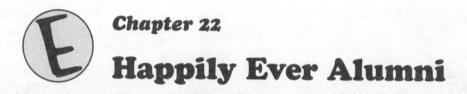

**Chapter 22**

# Happily Ever Alumni

Once you've received your diploma, packed your things, and left your college for the last time, you may think your affiliation with the institution is over. But for most students, this is not the case. Your college's alumni council will make a strong effort to keep in touch with you, and you should also value this connection. Alumni councils plan gatherings for alumni long after graduation, send out newsletters to update past students on changes in the college, and even offer help with finding jobs and graduate school programs.

## *Lifelong Affiliation*

Upon receiving your diploma, your name will be forever linked with your college. The college will benefit if you do well, touting you as an example of student success. Similarly, if the college is successful it reflects positively upon you. If your institution is receiving good press or developing a positive reputation amongst the general public, you'll be proud to call it your alma mater.

There are a variety of ways to show that you are proud of your college. You may wear a hat or jacket with your college logo. Perhaps you will wear a college sweatshirt when exercising, working around the yard, or while walking your dog. Many alumni also proudly display a college sticker somewhere in their cars, on the rear window or back bumper.

There are several ways to build a formal lifelong affiliation with your college, and one of the best is through participation in alumni leadership. For example, you could volunteer to become a contact person for your graduating class. This person coordinates the communication between individuals who have graduated and the college. This tends to be a low-stress but highly valuable role for a committed alumnus.

Your college may have an alumni council that gives you an opportunity to be more formally involved in the leadership of alumni and the college. Alumni councils assist with fundraising, distribute awards to alumni and undergraduates, and serve as a voice of alumni to the college. Such experiences tend to be very rewarding for council members, as well as very valuable for the college. You may be able to volunteer for a position on your school's alumni council, or you may have to be elected or chosen. However, most alumni councils lack sufficient support, and your services will most likely be very welcome.

# *Continuing Career Services*

It's a good idea to stay in touch with your college's career services office, especially if you plan to change jobs or careers several times throughout your life. You may also be able to stay in touch with an advisement office or counselor who guided you through your college career. Sometimes these offices will keep letters of recommendation from professors or other administrators on file for you well into the future.

Your career services staff will probably be willing to review your resume, even if your request comes long after your graduation. This is particularly useful if you are switching career fields, as each career area has its own idiosyncrasies. Your career services office can help present your education and experience in a way that will catch the attention of your target audience. As you gain more experience, you'll have to make decisions about which items to remove, which to keep, and how long to make your resume. Your career services office will help you with such decisions. If you cannot visit the office in person, it's worth asking if a career counselor can help you via e-mail or over the phone. A gathering of alumni in your local area might even choose to request a visit from a career services counselor. The college may be willing to pay for the counselor's travel expenses on such an occasion. Don't be afraid to make suggestions to your alumni council or to other college administrators; you are likely not the only alumnus with such an interest.

**FACT**

Some employers approach specific colleges when recruiting to fill open positions. Your school may list these companies on a career services Web site. These companies are a good place to start a job search, either right out of college or in the case of a job change. Your continued affiliation with your college gives you an advantage with these companies.

If you find that your first job out of college isn't what you hoped it would be, get in touch with your career services office. If possible, make an appointment and visit in person. Sit down with one of the career counselors and discuss your experiences and your expectations. You will want to discuss why your first job didn't work out as planned and what you have learned about yourself and your goals. A career counselor will help you sort out why things aren't going well and can direct you to the resources you need to search for a new career. Just as when you were an undergraduate these counselors have a variety of resources available, including surveys and books.

## *Making Donations*

The time will soon come when your college asks you for a donation. When this happens, keep two things in mind. First, almost no college education is paid for by the tuition and fees each student pays. The college, usually through endowment or state funds, subsidizes each student's education. In some cases, this is a dramatic subsidy, and students are rarely aware of this support. Second, your college education was an investment in your future, and your college helped you earn that education and loaned you the prestige of its reputation. Giving money is a very tangible show of support and appreciation for all that your college gave you. Donations to your alma mater will always be appreciated.

Your college is not looking to you for a major gift, at least not initially. Everyone knows that recent graduates are not earning a lot of money, are likely beginning to pay college loans, and are spending a lot of money organizing their lives. However, even a small gift is helpful to your college. Outside groups that evaluate colleges, and many organizations that rank colleges, look closely at alumni giving rates. These organizations are less interested in how much money alumni donate than how many alumni donate money.

Your college will establish different levels at which you can give in order to receive recognition. These levels are often given catchy names that attempt to reflect the generosity of the donor. "Friendship" level gifts may be anything under $100, "Bronze Circle" level gifts can be anything between $100 and $500, and "Presidential" level gifts anything over $10,000. Each college will set its own levels and titles for each level, enabling the college to recognize the generosity of all alumni and friends of the college. Donors at each level will be recognized in annual publications, which allows you to see your name in print and also see who else that you know is giving money to the school.

Many alumni receive annual phone calls from students working part-time for the college. This is a good chance for you to get information about your alma mater. Ask the student what activities she is involved with, what is going on around campus, and why she chose your college. And don't forget to make a pledge before you hang up.

You may want to direct your donation to a specific fund at the college. Some suggestions are:

- Athletics, or a particular athletic team
- A scholarship named for a favorite professor
- General financial aid based on need or merit
- Your favorite academic department
- Cocurricular groups, such as choirs or bands
- Student programming, or general support for clubs and organizations
- Campus buildings and grounds maintenance

Even if a fund does not exist to support your particular area of interest, be certain to tell the college what inspired you to make a donation. Your school wants your donation, but more importantly, they want your support.

## *Providing Internships*

Once you are out of college and established in a job, it's time to think about how you can help the undergraduates at your college. One of the easiest things for you to do is set up an internship for students from your school. This is a win-win situation. To start, the student will gain valuable experience and knowledge from working at your company for a summer or semester.

The student will also benefit from having an alumnus there to be a mentor, role model, and advocate. Next, the company will benefit by having a talented student work hard for its success. The company will also be able to advertise that it is committed to the education of young people, helping to train them for positions in the profession. Your company's public relations department can do a lot with the internship program and the connection between you and your alma mater. Finally, you will gain the appreciation of the student, potentially the respect and appreciation of your boss, and build a good connection with your school. Your college may want to write an article about you and the student in the alumni magazine.

If you're not able to set up an internship with your company, you may still be able to help students from your college. Many schools sponsor alumni-student networking which allows alumni to share career knowledge. By participating in this network, you can provide formal and informal advice to students, coach them in their job searches, and help them become successful professionals in your field. You may even be able to have a student shadow you for a day, demonstrating to him what your job is all about.

## Alumni Clubs

Your college probably has alumni around the country, and perhaps around the world. It's usually hard for these people to get back to campus regularly, yet they want to remain connected to the camaraderie and good times they knew as an undergraduate. As a response, your college may establish alumni clubs around the country. The benefits of these clubs include:

- Socializing with other alumni and friends of the college
- Occasional trips to local attractions and events
- Hearing from college representatives about happenings on campus
- Giving alumni a chance to have their voices heard by the college
- Opportunity to stay in touch with classmates
- Building professional networks
- Advice for alumni who are new to the area

If you settle in an area where there is no alumni club, contact your college and see what you can do to help start such an organization. If there are a fair number of alumni in your area, your inquiry is likely to be met with a lot of enthusiasm and perhaps even direct college support. You may be able to host the initial gathering at your home, or your alumni office may book space at a local hotel or club.

# Class Reunions and Alumni Publications

Colleges go out of their way to communicate with alumni. You will likely receive newsletters, magazines, and perhaps even e-mails from your alma mater. Initially, these may seem like junk mail to you because your college experience is so fresh in your mind. But as you move further from your graduation date you will value these communications. You will read about interesting events happening on campus, keep track of professors who are doing interesting work or are retiring, and see announcements from your classmates. It's always interesting to read about classmates who have married, had children, moved, or changed jobs.

You may find yourself inspired to write an article for one of your college's alumni publications. Consider writing about how your education has helped you achieve career and life goals. Or, write a piece about how one of your classmates is successful because of the experiences she had while at college. If you were part of a sports team, an RA, or held some other leadership position on campus write about how that experience helped you achieve your career goals. Even if your college can't use your article in its magazine, there is bound to be a use for it in other publications or as a testimonial on the college Web site.

As an undergraduate, you'll be aware of alumni coming back to campus for special events. Initially, these former students may represent an inconvenience to you, taking good parking spaces and creating longer lines at the bookstore. Later in your college career, you'll begin to see recent graduates you know and will get a chance to reconnect with them. As an alumnus, homecoming and other special events will represent an opportunity to get swept up in the excitement of college life once again. You'll also be able to share your college with your spouse and children.

**ALERT!**

Alumni publications can only reach you if you keep your college updated when you change addresses. Each time you move notify your alumni office of your new address, phone number, and e-mail account. This way, your college will be able to keep in touch with you and friends will use the alumni office to locate you when they lose touch.

Every few years during homecoming or alumni weekend, your class will have a reunion. These events will give you a chance to catch up with old friends, meet others' spouses or children, and reminisce about college experiences. Even if you suspect these events may be awkward or uncomfortable for you, take the chance and attend anyway. Once you arrive, you may see friends you had been missing, get a chance to speak with a favorite professor, and simply reconnect with your old self. Your life will change dramatically after college, and it will always be nice to look back on those years of good times and fond memories.

*Appendix*

# Internet Resources for College Students

There are numerous fun and useful Web sites for college students. From buying textbooks to keeping in touch with family at home there are resources on the Internet to help you with virtually any task or problem. Though you will certainly discover others during your college career, here are some Internet resources to give you a head start.

## *Academics*

**Sparknotes:** A collection of study guides, including literary and nonliterary topics

✑*www.sparknotes.com*

## *Humor and Games*

**The Onion:** A critically humorous news source

✑*www.theonion.com*

**FARK.com:** Obscure and unbelievable news stories

✑*www.fark.com*

**College Humor:** Amusing pictures, movies, and games

✑*www.collegehumor.com*

**Mad Blast:** Movies, music, television and games that parody popular figures

✑*www.MadBlast.com*

**JibJab:** Political parodies and cartoons

✑*www.jibjab.com*

**eBaum's World:** "Media for the masses": jokes, games, videos, and cartoons

✑*www.ebaumsworld.com*

**Homestarrunner:** Popular online cartoon

✑*www.homestarrunner.com*

**Bored.com:** Dedicated to procrastination and entertainment, with games, media, and links

✑*www.bored.com*

**Milk and Cookies:** Games and humorous news stories

✑*www.milkandcookies.com*

**Darwin Awards:** Honors those who improve the gene pool by removing themselves from it

✐*www.darwinawards.com*

# Personal Space on the Web

**Xanga.com:** "The Weblog Community"

✐*www.xanga.com*

**Livejournal:** A site for online journals

✐*www.livejournal.com*

**Angelfire:** Provides free web space

✐*www.angelfire.com*

**FreeWebs.com:** "The next generation of free web hosting"

✐*www.freewebs.com*

# Movies and Music

**IMDB:** The Internet movie database

✐*www.imdb.com*

**CMJ:** "New music first"; music reviews, reports, and news

✐*www.cmj.com*

**Pollstar:** Popular music resource

✐*www.pollstar.com*

**Allmusic:** A place to explore new bands or genres

✐*www.allmusic.com*

**Allmovie:** Film and actor reviews and movie sales

✐*www.allmovie.com*

## *Textbooks*

**Amazon.com:** Books, including new and used textbooks, and other products

   ✍*www.amazon.com*

**Barnes and Noble:** Books, including new and used textbooks, and other products

   ✍*www.barnesandnoble.com*

**Half.com:** An eBay partner site with new and used textbooks, as well as other products

   ✍*www.half.ebay.com*

**efollet:** Online location of a popular college bookstore

   ✍*www.efollett.com*

## *Travel*

**Student Universe:** A place to find cheap domestic and international flights, as well as resources for traveling in Europe

   ✍*www.studentuniverse.com*

**Lastminute.com:** A resource for travel within Europe

   ✍*www.lastminute.com*

**EasyJet.com:** Cheap travel within Europe and helpful to students studying abroad

   ✍*www.easyjet.com*

**Expedia Travel:** Flights, cruises, hotels, and travel packages

   ✍*www.expedia.com*

# E-Cards

**All 4 Free:** An Internet greeting card index
✍*www.rats2u.com*

**Hallmark.com:** The online site of the popular card and gift store
✍*www.hallmark.com*

# Other Interesting Sites

**Webshots:** A place to post photos for friends and family
✍*www.webshots.com*

**The Facebook:** An online directory connecting people through social networks at colleges
✍*www.thefacebook.com*

**Classmates.com:** An online database of high school graduates
✍*www.classmates.com*

***Consumer Reports:*** A nonprofit organization and print magazine with product reviews and other information
✍*www.consumerreports.org*

# Index

# THE EVERYTHING SERIES!

## BUSINESS & PERSONAL FINANCE

Everything® Budgeting Book
Everything® Business Planning Book
Everything® Coaching and Mentoring Book
Everything® Fundraising Book
Everything® Get Out of Debt Book
Everything® Grant Writing Book
Everything® Homebuying Book, 2nd Ed.
Everything® Homeselling Book
Everything® Home-Based Business Book
Everything® Investing Book
Everything® Landlording Book
Everything® Leadership Book
Everything® Managing People Book
Everything® Negotiating Book
Everything® Online Business Book
Everything® Personal Finance Book
Everything® Personal Finance in Your 20s
    and 30s Book
Everything® Project Management Book
Everything® Real Estate Investing Book
Everything® Robert's Rules Book, $7.95
Everything® Selling Book
Everything® Start Your Own Business Book
Everything® Wills & Estate Planning Book

## COOKING

Everything® Barbecue Cookbook
Everything® Bartender's Book, $9.95
Everything® Chinese Cookbook
Everything® College Cookbook
Everything® Cookbook
Everything® Diabetes Cookbook
Everything® Easy Gourmet Cookbook
Everything® Fondue Cookbook
Everything® Grilling Cookbook
Everything® Healthy Meals in Minutes
    Cookbook
Everything® Holiday Cookbook

Everything® Indian Cookbook
Everything® Low-Carb Cookbook
Everything® Low-Fat High-Flavor Cookbook
Everything® Low-Salt Cookbook
Everything® Meals for a Month Cookbook
Everything® Mediterranean Cookbook
Everything® Mexican Cookbook
Everything® One-Pot Cookbook
Everything® Pasta Cookbook
Everything® Quick Meals Cookbook
Everything® Slow Cooker Cookbook
Everything® Soup Cookbook
Everything® Thai Cookbook
Everything® Vegetarian Cookbook
Everything® Wine Book

## HEALTH

Everything® Alzheimer's Book
Everything® Diabetes Book
Everything® Hypnosis Book
Everything® Low Cholesterol Book
Everything® Massage Book
Everything® Menopause Book
Everything® Nutrition Book
Everything® Reflexology Book
Everything® Stress Management Book

## HISTORY

Everything® American Government Book
Everything® American History Book
Everything® Civil War Book
Everything® Irish History & Heritage Book
Everything® Middle East Book

## HOBBIES & GAMES

Everything® Blackjack Strategy Book
Everything® Brain Strain Book, $9.95
Everything® Bridge Book
Everything® Candlemaking Book

Everything® Card Games Book
Everything® Cartooning Book
Everything® Casino Gambling Book, 2nd Ed.
Everything® Chess Basics Book
Everything® Crossword and Puzzle Book
Everything® Crossword Challenge Book
Everything® Cryptograms Book, $9.95
Everything® Digital Photography Book
Everything® Drawing Book
Everything® Easy Crosswords Book
Everything® Family Tree Book
Everything® Games Book, 2nd Ed.
Everything® Knitting Book
Everything® Knots Book
Everything® Motorcycle Book
Everything® Online Genealogy Book
Everything® Photography Book
Everything® Poker Strategy Book
Everything® Pool & Billiards Book
Everything® Quilting Book
Everything® Scrapbooking Book
Everything® Sewing Book
Everything® Woodworking Book
Everything® Word Games Challenge Book

## HOME IMPROVEMENT

Everything® Feng Shui Book
Everything® Feng Shui Decluttering Book,
    $9.95
Everything® Fix-It Book
Everything® Homebuilding Book
Everything® Lawn Care Book
Everything® Organize Your Home Book

## EVERYTHING® KIDS' BOOKS

**All titles are $6.95**

Everything® Kids' Animal Puzzle & Activity
    Book
Everything® Kids' Baseball Book, 3rd Ed.

All Everything® books are priced at $12.95 or $14.95, unless otherwise stated. Prices subject to change without notice.

Everything® Kids' Bible Trivia Book
Everything® Kids' Bugs Book
Everything® Kids' Christmas Puzzle
    & Activity Book
Everything® Kids' Cookbook
Everything® Kids' Halloween Puzzle
    & Activity Book
Everything® Kids' Hidden Pictures Book
Everything® Kids' Joke Book
Everything® Kids' Knock Knock Book
Everything® Kids' Math Puzzles Book
Everything® Kids' Mazes Book
Everything® Kids' Money Book
Everything® Kids' Monsters Book
Everything® Kids' Nature Book
Everything® Kids' Puzzle Book
Everything® Kids' Riddles & Brain Teasers Book
Everything® Kids' Science Experiments Book
Everything® Kids' Sharks Book
Everything® Kids' Soccer Book
Everything® Kids' Travel Activity Book

## KIDS' STORY BOOKS

Everything® Bedtime Story Book
Everything® Fairy Tales Book

## LANGUAGE

Everything® Conversational Japanese Book
    (with CD), $19.95
Everything® French Phrase Book, $9.95
Everything® French Verb Book, $9.95
Everything® Inglés Book
Everything® Learning French Book
Everything® Learning German Book
Everything® Learning Italian Book
Everything® Learning Latin Book
Everything® Learning Spanish Book
Everything® Sign Language Book
Everything® Spanish Grammar Book
Everything® Spanish Phrase Book, $9.95
Everything® Spanish Verb Book, $9.95

## MUSIC

Everything® Drums Book (with CD), $19.95
Everything® Guitar Book
Everything® Home Recording Book
Everything® Playing Piano and Keyboards
    Book

Everything® Reading Music Book (with CD),
    $19.95
Everything® Rock & Blues Guitar Book
    (with CD), $19.95
Everything® Songwriting Book

## NEW AGE

Everything® Astrology Book
Everything® Dreams Book, 2nd Ed.
Everything® Ghost Book
Everything® Love Signs Book, $9.95
Everything® Numerology Book
Everything® Paganism Book
Everything® Palmistry Book
Everything® Psychic Book
Everything® Reiki Book
Everything® Spells & Charms Book
Everything® Tarot Book
Everything® Wicca and Witchcraft Book

## PARENTING

Everything® Baby Names Book
Everything® Baby Shower Book
Everything® Baby's First Food Book
Everything® Baby's First Year Book
Everything® Birthing Book
Everything® Breastfeeding Book
Everything® Father-to-Be Book
Everything® Father's First Year Book
Everything® Get Ready for Baby Book
Everything® Getting Pregnant Book
Everything® Homeschooling Book
Everything® Parent's Guide to Children
    with ADD/ADHD
Everything® Parent's Guide to Children
    with Asperger's Syndrome
Everything® Parent's Guide to Children
    with Autism
Everything® Parent's Guide to Children
    with Dyslexia
Everything® Parent's Guide to Positive
    Discipline
Everything® Parent's Guide to Raising a
    Successful Child
Everything® Parent's Guide to Tantrums
Everything® Parent's Guide to the Overweight
    Child
Everything® Parenting a Teenager Book
Everything® Potty Training Book, $9.95

Everything® Pregnancy Book, 2nd Ed.
Everything® Pregnancy Fitness Book
Everything® Pregnancy Nutrition Book
Everything® Pregnancy Organizer, $15.00
Everything® Toddler Book
Everything® Tween Book
Everything® Twins, Triplets, and More Book

## PETS

Everything® Cat Book
Everything® Dachshund Book, $12.95
Everything® Dog Book
Everything® Dog Health Book
Everything® Dog Training and Tricks Book
Everything® Golden Retriever Book, $12.95
Everything® Horse Book
Everything® Labrador Retriever Book, $12.95
Everything® Poodle Book, $12.95
Everything® Pug Book, $12.95
Everything® Puppy Book
Everything® Rottweiler Book, $12.95
Everything® Tropical Fish Book

## REFERENCE

Everything® Car Care Book
Everything® Classical Mythology Book
Everything® Computer Book
Everything® Divorce Book
Everything® Einstein Book
Everything® Etiquette Book
Everything® Mafia Book
Everything® Philosophy Book
Everything® Psychology Book
Everything® Shakespeare Book

## RELIGION

Everything® Angels Book
Everything® Bible Book
Everything® Buddhism Book
Everything® Catholicism Book
Everything® Christianity Book
Everything® Jewish History & Heritage Book
Everything® Judaism Book
Everything® Koran Book
Everything® Prayer Book
Everything® Saints Book
Everything® Torah Book
Everything® Understanding Islam Book

All Everything® books are priced at $12.95 or $14.95, unless otherwise stated. Prices subject to change without notice.

Everything® World's Religions Book
Everything® Zen Book

## SCHOOL & CAREERS

Everything® Alternative Careers Book
Everything® College Survival Book, 2nd Ed.
Everything® Cover Letter Book, 2nd Ed.
Everything® Get-a-Job Book
Everything® Job Interview Book
Everything® New Teacher Book
Everything® Online Job Search Book
Everything® Paying for College Book
Everything® Practice Interview Book
Everything® Resume Book, 2nd Ed.
Everything® Study Book

## SELF-HELP

Everything® Great Sex Book
Everything® Kama Sutra Book
Everything® Self-Esteem Book

## SPORTS & FITNESS

Everything® Fishing Book
Everything® Fly-Fishing Book
Everything® Golf Instruction Book

Everything® Pilates Book
Everything® Running Book
Everything® Total Fitness Book
Everything® Weight Training Book
Everything® Yoga Book

## TRAVEL

Everything® Family Guide to Hawaii
Everything® Family Guide to New York City, 2nd Ed.
Everything® Family Guide to RV Travel & Campgrounds
Everything® Family Guide to the Walt Disney World Resort®, Universal Studios®, and Greater Orlando, 4th Ed.
Everything® Family Guide to Washington D.C., 2nd Ed.
Everything® Guide to Las Vegas
Everything® Guide to New England
Everything® Travel Guide to the Disneyland Resort®, California Adventure®, Universal Studios®, and the Anaheim Area

## WEDDINGS

Everything® Bachelorette Party Book, $9.95
Everything® Bridesmaid Book, $9.95

Everything® Elopement Book, $9.95
Everything® Father of the Bride Book, $9.95
Everything® Groom Book, $9.95
Everything® Mother of the Bride Book, $9.95
Everything® Wedding Book, 3rd Ed.
Everything® Wedding Checklist, $9.95
Everything® Wedding Etiquette Book, $7.95
Everything® Wedding Organizer, $15.00
Everything® Wedding Shower Book, $7.95
Everything® Wedding Vows Book, $7.95
Everything® Weddings on a Budget Book, $9.95

## WRITING

Everything® Creative Writing Book
Everything® Get Published Book
Everything® Grammar and Style Book
Everything® Guide to Writing a Book Proposal
Everything® Guide to Writing a Novel
Everything® Guide to Writing Children's Books
Everything® Screenwriting Book
Everything® Writing Poetry Book
Everything® Writing Well Book

· · · · · · · · · · · · · · · · · · · · · · · · · · · · · · · · · · · · · · · · · · · · · · · · · · · ·

## We have Everything® for the beginner crafter!
### All titles are $14.95

Everything® Crafts—Baby Scrapbooking
1-59337-225-6

Everything® Crafts—Bead Your Own Jewelry
1-59337-142-X

Everything® Crafts—Create Your Own Greeting Cards
1-59337-226-4

Everything® Crafts—Easy Projects
1-59337-298-1

Everything® Crafts—Polymer Clay for Beginners
1-59337-230-2

Everything® Crafts—Rubber Stamping Made Easy
1-59337-229-9

Everything® Crafts—Wedding Decorations and Keepsakes
1-59337-227-2

Available wherever books are sold!
To order, call 800-872-5627, or visit us at *www.everything.com*
Everything® and everything.com® are registered trademarks of F+W Publications, Inc.